THE SHEFFIE...

Printed & Published by:

ALD Design & Print
279 Sharrow Vale Road
Sheffield S11 8ZF
Great Britain
Tel: 0114 267 9402

First Published September 2002

ISBN 1-901587-24-X

THE SHEFFIELD HANGED

Being an account of those hanged
for Sheffield Crimes between 1750 and 1864

DAVID BENTLEY

Alistair Lofthouse DESIGN PRINT &

Other Titles by the same Author

Select Cases from the Twelve Judges' Notebooks

English Criminal Justice in the Nineteenth Century

Victorian Men of Law

About the Author

David Bentley is a circuit judge. Born in Sheffield and educated at King Edward VII School, Sheffield, University College, London and the University of Sheffield, he practised at the bar in Sheffield from 1969 until his appointment to the bench in 1988. He took silk in 1984. He has a doctorate in nineteenth-century legal history and is the author of books and articles on the subject. He lives in Sheffield with his wife and two sons.

Other titles in the series:

Contents

Page

Foreword

The cover illustration is Thomas Rowlandson's painting *Mary Evans hung at York August 10, 1799 for poisoning her husband.* The title is puzzling, for no woman of that name was executed at York in 1799 or in any other year. The only women put to death at York Tyburn in the 1790s were Elizabeth Elliot in 1792 and Ann Scalbert in 1794 and since neither had murdered her husband it seems unlikely that either is the woman in the picture. Whoever she was, she is but minutes away from death. Her hands clasped in front of her, she is earnestly joining in the prayers the chaplain is reciting while the coarse-featured hangman (a convict from the county gaol if this be, indeed, a York hanging) adjusts the noose. She has yet to be pinioned but, as soon as she has been, she will be turned off. If she dies instantaneously she will be fortunate. More likely she will slowly strangle with her body convulsed in agony. If she takes a long time to die and the hangman is feeling merciful, he may pull on her legs to shorten her death throes, no doubt to the accompaniment of coarse ribaldry from the crowd. After an hour her body will be cut down and handed over to the York county hospital for dissection. That is what happened to young Mary Thorpe of Ecclesfield in March, 1800 and between 1750 and 1864 no fewer than 28 other Sheffielders died a similarly painful and shameful death on the York scaffold.

In 1864 Leeds was made Assize town for the West Riding which meant that henceforth all executions of West Riding criminals would take place not at York but outside Armley prison Leeds. Leeds, in fact, only ever staged one public hanging before the coming into force of the Capital Punishment Amendment Act, 1868 which required executions to be carried out within prisons out of public view. That execution was of two south Yorkshire men, Sheffielder Joseph Myers and Rotherham born James Sargisson, in September 1864.

This book tells the stories of those hanged at York and Leeds between 1750 and 1864 for Sheffield crimes. The legal process from arrest to execution is described in detail as are the crimes which earned the hanged their 'free ride to York.' The sites of the various York gallows and the route followed by the execution cart on its way to Tyburn are given, not least because there is little information to be had about them in York guide books.

Two Sheffield men who deserve more than the passing mention they receive in the text are James Montgomery and William Overend. Montgomery, the editor of the *Sheffield Iris*, was twice imprisoned in York castle at the end of the eighteenth century. During his incarceration he wrote *'Prison Amusements,'* a book of poems in which he describes his experiences. Extracts from it are included in appendix 3. William Overend QC, son of the Sheffield surgeon, Hall Overend, was one of the leading barristers of his day and beyond doubt the finest advocate Sheffield produced in the nineteenth century. His powerful closing speech to the jury in the Waddington murder case will leave the reader in no doubt as to his ability.

I would like to thank the staff of the York Castle Museum and the York and Sheffield Local Studies Libraries for invaluable assistance generously given. I am grateful to my friend Judge Patrick Robertshaw for reading the text and making valuable suggestions for its improvement.

David Bentley

CHAPTER ONE

The Road to the Scaffold

Arrest and committal for trial

For eighteenth-century Sheffield criminals the journey to the gallows began in the Town Hall cells: for it was here that those taken on suspicion of felony[1] were lodged to await examination by a magistrate.[2]

The Town Hall, a mean soot-blackened brick building, stood at the south-east corner of the parish churchyard.[3] Square to the points of the compass, with its east wall facing High Street and its south-east corner and southern wall projecting a considerable distance into Church Lane, (now Church Street), it was a serious obstruction to traffic. Erected by the Town Trustees in 1700 as a court-house and town meeting place, it had two floors and a pitched roof, astride which sat a belfry topped by a gilded ball. On the first floor was a dismal hall. There was matting on the floor, a table made out of three deal boards covered in green baize and the town chest.[4] The royal arms on the wall opposite the entrance offered the only hint that it served as a courtroom.[5] Its normal use was as a magistrates' or petty sessions court and as the meeting place of the Town Trustees, but every third year the West Riding Quarter Sessions sat there. Occasionally, it was hired out for dancing and auction sales[6] and once a dinner was given there in honour of Lady Howard, the mother of the Duke of Norfolk.

---

[1] At common law felonies were 'venomous crimes' conviction for which resulted in an automatic forfeiture of all the felon's property to the Crown. They also cost him his life, all felonies, with the exception of petty larceny, being capital. As a result of the fondness of eighteenth-century parliaments for the death penalty by 1800 the number of felonies stood at close to 200.

[2] Either detained at the scene of the crime by local people or tracked down by the constable they would end up in his hands and would be taken by him to the Town Hall cells.

[3] Now the Cathedral churchyard.

[4] The chief treasure contained in the chest was a copy of the Town Burgesses' grant to Thomas Duke of Norfolk and a note from the Duke to the Burgesses for £100.

[5] The entrance to the hall, which was on the High Street side of the building, was reached by a flight of steps. At election time parliamentary candidates used the steps to address electors.

[6] In 1727 Richard Snell paid 7s for the use of the hall for seven weeks for dancing.

On the ground floor, on the High Street side of the building were shops, behind which was a narrow passageway with three cells running off it.[7] Dark and cramped (eight foot square by six foot high), with an open sewer running along one wall. The accommodation they provided was grim but no worse than that in most town lock-ups.

Mercifully the sojourn there of those taken for felony was usually short. It was the duty of the constable to bring them before a magistrate for examination as soon as reasonably possible and magistrates sat in the town most days.

The magistrate's examination was not a trial (magistrates had no power to try felony); its purpose was firstly, to record the evidence against the accused and secondly, to determine whether that evidence was sufficient to justify sending him to the county Assizes for trial. The witnesses in support of the charge were called in turn and questioned on oath by the magistrate or his clerk, the accused having the right to cross-examine. The evidence of each was taken down in the form of a written deposition, which he would be required to sign before leaving the witness box. Once the prosecutor's witnesses had been heard, the accused would be called on by the magistrate for his defence. It had, by as early as 1730 become customary to warn prisoners that they were not obliged to say anything. Having listened to his account, if any, the magistrate had next to decide whether to send him for trial. Dalton's *Countrey Justice* and Burn's *Justice of the Peace,* the text-books upon which all magistrates' clerks relied for their law, were uncompromising in their advice: 'even though it shall appear to the Justice that the Prisoner is not guilty [the best and safest course is to commit him] for it is not fit that a Man once arrested and charged with Felony (or suspicion thereof) should be delivered upon any Man's Discretion, without Further Trial.' It was guidance which the Rev. Wilkinson, Vicar of Sheffield and magistrate for the town, would (from what we know of him) have been likely to follow to the letter.

Those sent for trial were committed to the county gaol, it being settled practice not to grant bail to those capitally accused.

---

[7] In the late eighteenth century the cell area was commonly known as Sam Hall's parlour, after the jailor.

Prisoners who appeared for preliminary examination rarely had the means to employ a lawyer but many country benches in any event refused to admit attorneys, regarding their presence as an obstruction to justice. This unsatisfactory state of affairs continued until 1836 when prisoners were by statute granted the right to legal representation.

Examinations in felony cases were normally held in the hall above the cells but, by the 1790s, the magistrates were also using the ground floor of the Cutlers' Hall, on the opposite side of Church Lane, as an over-spill court. When this was in use, the prisoners who were to appear there that day would be marshalled in chained gangs in the churchyard and taken across in batches as their cases were called on.

At the end of each day's sitting those prisoners sentenced to imprisonment by the magistrates or remanded by them in custody to await trial at the West Riding Quarter Sessions, would be chained together and marched off in the custody of the town beadle to the House of Correction at Wakefield. As they toiled up Pye Bank their relatives and friends would be waiting to pass them drink and comforts. It is possible that those committed to the county gaol at York also had to walk but it is more likely that they were conveyed there by cart, since to march capital prisoners such a long distance on foot, even heavily shackled, would have involved an obvious security risk.[8] The route followed was along the Wicker, through Attercliffe to Doncaster and thence to York via the great north road.

Where the charge against a man was homicide there would, in addition to the hearing before the magistrate, be a coroner's inquest, the purpose of which was to establish the identity of the deceased and the cause of death. Depositions would be taken from all persons who had relevant evidence to give. The accused, if present, had the right to give evidence and might himself be permitted to put questions. If the inquest jury returned a verdict of murder or manslaughter against the accused, the coroner would commit him for trial, even where he already stood committed by a

---

[8] Newspapers are silent on the matter. We know, however, that transports (persons sentenced to transportation) were conveyed to their port of embarkation by wagon: see e.g. *Sheffield Local Register*, April 24, 1747 'Three wagons loaded with the rebels brought through the town and removed the following day being ordered for transportation.'

magistrate. Inquests were at this time commonly held in public houses or a public building close to where the body had been found.

At the start of the nineteenth century there were moves afoot to have the Town Hall pulled down. Wilkinson and his fellow magistrates petitioned the West Riding Quarter Sessions to help defray the cost of a new building to be erected on Castle Hill 'on the outskirts of the town'[9] The existing town hall was, they complained, unfit for the transaction of court business and its prison wretched and incapable of improvement. After a good deal of wrangling as to who should pay, the scheme was eventually agreed. The work was completed in 1808 at a cost of £5,600. The new Town Hall, which stood at the corner of Castle Street and Waingate, contained two court-rooms, a cell area and offices. It quickly became too small to serve the needs of the growing town and in 1833 it was extended. Because of poor design its cells were not escape proof and, during the course of the nineteenth century, there were several spectacular break-outs.[10] When John Joseph Gurney and his sister, Elizabeth Fry, viewed them in September 1818 (only ten years after they were built) they were in a foul state:

> '[There is] a lock house under the Town Hall consisting of a small court in which, on account of its insecurity, the prisoners were not allowed to take exercise, and four cells measuring respectively ten feet square These cells are fitted up with raised platforms on which is placed the bedding, that is some straw and two rugs in each cell; they are tolerably ventilated and warmed by flues but were, when we saw them, in a state of very great filth... The court-yard might at trifling expense be rendered so secure as to afford ... the opportunity of air and exercise.'[11]

---

[9] A memorial was presented to the County Quarter Sessions by Rev Wilkinson and three other magistrates who commonly sat in the town, drawing attention to the deficiencies of the town hall and recommending that it be pulled down and replaced by a new building which it was proposed be erected at Castle Hill and towards the cost of which the Duke of Norfolk willing to make a contribution. They pointed to the very inconvenient construction and miserable state of the Sessions House at Sheffield 'which is wanting of every necessary accommodation for the magistrates, jury and other officers of the court and to the very wretched condition of the Riding Prisons at Sheffield which are not only fit at present for the purposes to which they are applied but are incapable of being rendered so by any repair or improvement that can be made to them in their present situation which is itself inconvenient being in the centre of the Town and obstructing the free passage into one of the principal streets and narrowing the approach to the Parish Church whereas the proposed site of the intended new building is most conveniently situated at the outskirts of the town.' After a good deal of wrangling about how the cost should be shared, approval was eventually given and the new Town Hall, with ample cell accommodation, was erected at the junction of Castle Street and Waingate. The cost was £5,600 of which Duke of Norfolk £2,950 Town Trustees £1,000 Cutlers' Company £500.
[10] For details see D. Bentley, *Victorian Men of Law*, ALD, Sheffield, 2000, p. 97 n. 3.
[11] John Joseph Gurney, *Notes on a visit made to some of the Prisons in Scotland and the North of England in the company of Elizabeth Fry*, 2nd ed, Longman Hurst, London, 1819, p 82-83.

Forty years on things had not improved. 'The Town Hall cells,' wrote Pawson & Brailsford in their 1862 *Illustrated Guide to Sheffield and its Neighbourhood:*

> 'are confined, partly underground and most unhealthy. It is not unfrequent, when prisoners are confined here for any length of time, pending the preliminary enquiry before the magistrates, for them to beg to be removed to the Wakefield House of Correction, in order to escape the discomfort and unhealthiness of the local prison.'

By the date that this was written those committed or remanded to Wakefield no longer had to walk but were conveyed there in open wagon.

Confined in the county gaol

Prisoners sent to York for trial were, on arrival in the city, lodged in the county gaol to await the coming of the Assize judges.

In the seventeenth and eighteenth centuries gaols were run as profit making concerns with the gaoler, whose office carried no salary, living off the fees exacted from prisoners and the profits made from trading with them.[12] So lucrative were gaoler-ships that until 1730, when their sale was prohibited, they were regularly bought and sold.

The fees which could be demanded of prisoners:

> 'varied from gaol to gaol and rested on ancient custom, which had usually been embodied in a detailed table, authorised or ratified by the local justices ... Every incident in the prison life, from admission to discharge, was made the occasion of a fee.'[13]

---

[12] Ultimate responsibility for the county gaol lay with the sheriff who could be punished by the Crown in the event of an escape. Beyond taking a bond of indemnification from the gaoler as protection against the legal consequences of escapes, most sheriffs took little or no interest in the gaol leaving the gaoler to run it as he saw fit. In the late seventeenth century the county magistrates were given statutory power to repair gaols and in the eighteenth limited powers to control the way they were run and managed.

[13] S & B Webb, *English Prisons under Local Government*, Longmans, London 1922, p. 5.

But fees were only part of the gaoler's profits. The fact that he exercised uncontrolled power over his prisoners gave him unlimited opportunities for extortion. If a prisoner had the money he could buy all manner of comforts and privileges: lighter fetters, better accommodation, food, ale, kindling, a bed, bedding, amusements such as skittles and playing cards and ready access to friends and family. In this way the well-to-do could buy their way out of the squalor and misery which were the lot of poor prisoners, spending their time instead in comparative comfort. To extortion was added a yet further misery - garnish (the cruel custom 'which compelled every newcomer to pay a stated sum to be spent by the whole community in drink. If the unfortunate victim was unable or unwilling to pay, he was stripped of his clothing or made to run the gauntlet')[14]

In York, the Castle was the county gaol, as it had been since at least the thirteenth century. In the seventeenth century, like the other northern gaols, it enjoyed a foul reputation and high mortality.[15] Substantially rebuilt in 1480 after its foundations had been undermined by the river, it had over the following centuries fallen into disrepair. In July 1658 the county had been presented at the summer assizes for the insufficiency of the gaol but nothing was done. By the 1670s it was largely in ruins with the prisoners by now confined in two of the surviving towers. Conditions inside were grim with debtors and male and female felons herded together without discrimination. Denied the ordinary conveniences and necessities of life, inmates were entirely at the mercy of the gaolers for their food and for everything they possessed. How comfortable or wretched a life a remand prisoner had depended on the depth of his purse. Those without money had to subsist on the county allowance, a small ration of bread paid for out of the proceeds of a rate levied by the county magistrates. Prisoners with money, however, lived in relative comfort; they could buy whatever food and liquor they

---

[14] S. & B. Webb, op.cit., pp 24-25. When John Howard visited York in 1774 he found that garnish had been abolished at the Castle that year: John Howard, *The State of the Prisons in England and Wales*, 4th edn, 1792, pp 405-07.

[15] Twyford & Griffith, *The Records of York Castle*, Griffiths and Farran, London, 1880, p. 137 'The number of prisoners who died in York Castle Prison during (the seventeenth century) was positively startling. [At that period] all prisoners dying a natural death were buried in the Churchyard of St Mary [Castlegate] and from a perusal of parish registers dating from 1604 it would appear that 16 was the maximum in any one month, and, on an average of 25 years, there were about 30 per annum.

desired and might even be allowed out into the city of an evening (under escort) to visit playhouses, taverns and coffee houses or to dine with friends. A petition of 1658 complaining of abuse of office by the keepers of the gaol alleged that this latter privilege had even been extended to men 'condemned for high treason, murther [and] for felony in execution.' The keeper's liberality in the matter of jaunts of this kind was, as the petition makes clear, matched by his rapacity in the matter of fees:

> 'The gaoler [hath] contrary to a table of several fees and Acts of Parliament ... demaunded and taken severall sums of money for chambers rent and likewise for our own beds and bedding and doth compell us to pay for ease of irons, altho' we have paid the summe to the former jailer to whom we were committed... [and hath] tak[en] unjust fees from the prisoners when discharged receiving £16 and 8s from 6 men committed and indicted for High Treason at the last Assizes as fees due to ... besides £6 for ease of irons, [he or his] friends taking or receiving money at several times from persons indicted for murther at lent Assizes last promising that they jury should acquitt.' [16]

In 1700 the county magistrates at long last decided that something must be done about the jail. Availing themselves of the provisions of the recently enacted Gaol Act, they pulled down the towers and erected a new gaol in their stead. Financed by a rate of three pence in the pound upon all lands in the county, the work, begun in 1701, was completed four years later. Built with stone taken from the ruins of St Mary's Abbey, the new prison consisted of a central block with two projecting wings, each of which was approached by a staircase.[17] Handsomely appointed and standing opposite Clifford's Tower, it was much praised. Defoe thought it 'the most stately and complete

---

[16] Surtees Society, Vol 40, *York Castle Depositions* (Frances Andrews, Durham,, 1861), xxxii.

[17] The central block was and still is topped by a clock tower. The clock, made by John Terry of York in 1716, originally had only one hand but in 1854 it was fitted with two. (T.P. Cooper, *The History of York Castle*, 1911, p 214). It inspired the following lines by the Sheffield poet James Montgomery:

> 'How proudly shines the crazy clock
> A clock whose wheels eccentric run
> More like my head than like the sun
> And yet it shews us right or wrong
> The days are only twelve hours long
> Tho' captives often reckon here
> Each day a month each month a year'

of any in the whole Kingdom if not Europe.' This was also opinion of John Wesley[18] and Smollett.[19]

The ground floor was given over to felons; the cells for male felons were in the west wing, and those for condemned prisoners,[20] female felons and recalcitrant debtors in the east wing, to the rear of the governor's apartments. The two upper floors housed debtors and also contained further apartments for the governor and a large chapel.[21] At the side of the west wing was a half-moon shaped exercise yard for transports[22] which was also used for unshackling. The area between the two wings was enclosed with railings and served as an airing yard for the felons. Debtors (except for those confined on the felons' floor) were until 1835 permitted to roam with the deer over the Castle Green all day.[23]

For all the building's architectural splendours, the regime inside was still bleak and miserable for remand prisoners without means.[24] When John Howard,[25] the prison reformer, visited the prison in 1774 he noted that whilst rooms in the debtors' section were airy and healthy the accommodation for male felons was poor:

---

[18] Wesley records in his diary for July 19, 1759 'I visited two prisoners in the Castle which I suppose must be the most commodious prison in Europe' (cited by Cooper, op. cit., p 216)

[19] T. Smollett, *The Exoedition of Humphry Clinker* (Wordsworth edn. 1995), p 167 'the best, in all respects, I ever saw at home or abroad.'

[20] The largest of the condemned cells, named after the jailor, was known as Pompey's Parlour.

[21] The male prisoners sat along the wall; female prisoners in front of the pulpit, the keeper, visitors and debtors in a gallery.

[22] I.e. persons sentenced to transportation.

[23] A. W. Twford and Major Arthur Griffiths, op. cit., p 149.

[24] Nonetheless conditions in the Castle were infinitely superior to those in the York City gaol where the city prisoners were held; see a letter dated February 14, 1746 from the Archbishop of York Lord Chancellor Hardwicke (cited in P.C. Yorke, *The Life of Lord Chancellor Hardwicke*, Cambridge University Press, 1913, i, 501):

> '...it behoves the judge that comes the circuit to look to that matter of the jail. The prisoners die and the Recorder told me yesterday when the turnkey opens the cells in the morning the steam and stench is intolerable and scarce credible. The very walls are covered with lice in the room over which the Grand Jury sit.'

[25] **John Howard** (1726-90), captured and imprisoned in France, he devoted his life to informing the public of the foul and degrading state of English prisons. Published *State of the Prisons*, 1777, an *Appendix* thereto 1780 and a new version with further evidence in 1784. Also travelled abroad to survey foreign prisons.

The felons' courtyard .. is too small and has no water... The day room for men is only twenty-six feet by eight.' In it are three cells; in another place nine cells, and three in another. The cells are in general about seven feet and a half by six and a half, and eight and a half high, close and dark, having only either a hole above the door about four inches by eight, or some other perforations in the door of about an inch in diameter; not any of them to the open air but into passages or entries. In most of these cells three prisoners are locked up at night, in winter for fourteen to sixteen hours; straw on the stone floors; no bedsteads. There are four condemned rooms about seven feet square. A sewer in one of the passages often makes these parts of the gaol very offensive and I cannot say they are clean.

Spending long hours locked up in a dark overcrowded cell was but one of the hardships which untried prisoners had to endure. Their lives were unremittingly bleak: constantly shackled, poorly fed, unable to keep themselves clean and with thoughts of the gallows never far away.

To reduce the risk of being called upon to indemnify the sheriff against the consequences of escape, gaolers routinely ironed their charges. But for all this, escapes from county gaols were far from rare. In 1761 twenty French prisoners escaped from York castle. Four years later the felons rose up against the gaolers and would have escaped had the debtors not come to the assistance of the prison staff.

The only food provided was still the county allowance which by now consisted of 2½ lb of bread a day and 6d a week to spend on other food such as potatoes.[26] This was, as an apothecary acknowledged in 1822, little better than a starvation diet. The county magistrates had statutory power to levy a rate for the purpose of purchasing materials with which to set poor prisoners to work, thereby giving them a means of earning money. They chose not to exercise it, no doubt considering the county allowance a sufficient provision. As a result inmates spent their days in idleness.[27]

---

[26] Howard, op cit, lists five charities established for the relief of prisoners in the Castle; they yielded £7 a year plus further sums to be spent on the provision of bread and rushes.

[27] When John Joseph Gurney and his sister Elizabeth Fry visited the Castle in 1818 they noted that prisoners who were unable to read for the most part received no instruction whatever although they were heartened by information given to them by the Revd Richardson, a York clergyman:

York, November 24, 1818

'About three years ago some boys from Sheffield were tried and condemned at York for robbing a watchmaker or silversmith's shop and left for transportation. One of the magistrates who was of the grand jury struck with compassion for the youths and the miserable appearance of these poor culprits spoke to them after their conviction and on his return to his own seat in the country wrote

The lack of running water meant that it was difficult for prisoners to keep themselves or their clothes clean. Nor did acquittal by itself end a prisoner's sufferings; the gaoler and the clerk of assize were each entitled to be paid a discharge fee and an acquitted defendant would not be released until these had been paid.[28]

As in all prisons in all ages, time weighed heavily on the hands of those confined in the Castle, and for none more so than those committed just after an assize had ended, who faced a wait of at least six months before they took their trials. The chapel services (prayers were held five times a week and on Thursday and Sunday there was a sermon) afforded some relief from the tedium but for the rest of the time, there being no work provided, inmates were left to their own devices.

In theory, an untried prisoner could use his time preparing his defence. Reality was somewhat different. Until 1836 the law denied an accused copies of the depositions taken at his committal. Hence, unless he had taken his own note of the evidence or paid an attorney to take one for him, he would have only his recollection of what the prosecution witnesses had said to rely on and, if he was illiterate, as most prisoners were, there could be no question of writing down notes of questions to ask or points to make; he would have to keep everything in his head. Prisoners, whose homes were far from York, had the added problem of trying to contact and secure the attendance at court of witnesses whose evidence might help their case. Even if the witnesses could be contacted, unless they could afford to pay for their own transport or were prepared

---

to the Governor of York Castle expressing a wish that some useful instruction might be afforded to them while they remained there promising to bear the expense of it and desiring him to consult with me on the subject. It occurred to me that the best thing to be done was to establish a school in which the boys might be regularly taught. The governor was kind enough to furnish a proper room; a decent young man (a prisoner for debt) who had been the master of a cheap school in the north of Yorkshire was hired to teach this little school and I undertook that my curate and I would inspect it. The project succeeded beyond our expectations. The master soon grew fond of his pupils on account of their rapid improvement in reading writing, etc. The boys were diligent and attentive to instruction happy and orderly; their behaviour at the chapel and their whole conduct at other times gave us pleasure. This continued till the time of their departure from the castle.'

J.J. Gurney, op. cit, p 7.

[28] In force when John Howard visited York in the 1770s was a table of fees approved by the Assize Judges at the summer Assize 1735. This required every acquitted or discharged prisoner to pay a discharge fee to the gaoler. The discharge fee for acquitted prisoners was 6s 8d and 2s to the turnkeys; for prisoners against whom no bill was found it was 2s and for those convicted but later pardoned it was 7s.6. and 2s to the turnkeys: J Howard, op. cit., 4th edn, 1792, pp. 405-07. The discharge fees due to the Clerk of Assize were £1.5.s.4d from an acquitted prisoner and 14s. 8d from those discharged - Howard, op. cit., Table V.

to walk, there was no way of getting them to court.

By 1779 the prison was badly overcrowded and the grand jury made a presentment that it was insufficient (with 83 inmates it had more prisoners than any county gaol other than Newgate). The county magistrates immediately gave authority for its enlargement. In 1780 a further prison building was erected at right angles to and to the north east of the gaol. Enlarged by the Atkinsons in 1803, as well as providing additional cells, it also housed offices for the clerk of Assize, a record repository and cells and day rooms for prisoners. To this new block, which came to be known as the Female prison, female felons, misdemeanants and some debtors were transferred leaving the central block for male felons and the bulk of the debtors.

Also, Parliament by now was beginning to bestir itself to deal with the problem of prison conditions. In 1773 county magistrates were empowered to provide chaplains for gaols and in the following year 'the mortality caused by gaol fever ... produced an Act empowering the justices to take measures for cleansing the gaols and the prisoners.' [29]

---

[29] Because of the fear of catching disease from the inmates, magistrates and gaolers rarely ventured on tours of inspection themselves: see Howard, op cit., p 37 'many of the oldest [gaolers] have answered 'none of those gentlemen [i.e. magistrates] ever looked into the dungeon or even the wards of my gaol.' Others have said 'Those gentlemen think that if they come into my gaol they would soon be in their grave.' In my first journey many county gaolers excused themselves from going with me into the felons' ward...and p 27 'In York castle in 1774 the felons told me over and again that the gaoler had not been in their ward for months. I would not have quoted a report from felons if the turnkey who was present had not confirmed their testimony.'

Old Town Hall - Identifiable by the belfry on its pitched roof, the Old Town Hall built in 1700 was until its demolition a serious obstruction to traffic. The court-room was on the first floor.

New Town Hall - Opened in 1807, with cells beneath, it served during the 19th century as both magistrates' and Quarter Sessions court-house.

The county gaol 1728. The building on the left is the moot hall;
the one on the right the grand jury house.

The county gaol c. 1750. Note the staircases (now demolished)
and the grill enclosing the felons' yard.

Condemned cell – York castle.

The new prison erected 1826-35 and demolished 1935.

The Assizes Courts, York Castle erected 1777. Note the statue of justice standing atop the pediment, alluded to by James Montgomery in 'The Pleasures of Imprisonment, Epistle II.'

1774 also saw the enactment of the Discharged Prisoners Act, which required the county to pay the gaol fees of all acquitted prisoners who were to be set free in open court.[30] In 1815 Bennet's Act imposed a total prohibition upon the taking of gaol fees: gaolers who had hitherto been remunerated in whole or part by fees were henceforth to be paid by salary.

---

[30] 14 Geo III c. 20. Howard noted that even after acquitted prisoners had been relieved of gaolers' fees by statute, if they failed to pay the fees due to the Clerk of Assize (as to which see n 28 above) they would in some places find themselves detained until the judges left town. He says at p. 15 'I was informed at Durham that Judge Gould, at the assize 1775, laid a fine of fifty pounds on the gaoler for detaining some acquitted prisoners for the fees of the clerk of assize. But on the intercession of the Bishop (proprietor of the gaol) the fine was remitted; and the prisoners set at large: the judge ordering the clerk of assize to explain to him in London the foundation of the demand. One pretence for detaining acquitted prisoners is, that 'It is possible other indictments may be laid against them before the judge leaves town.' I call it a pretence as the grand jury are often dismissed some days before that time, and because those who do satisfy the demands of the clerk of assize are immediately discharged. Another pretence is: the gaoler tells you 'he takes them back to knock off their irons.' But this may be done in court: in London they have an engine or block by the help of which they take off the irons with ease in a minute.'

Peel's Gaol Act of 1823 was even more far reaching, defining the legal duties of prison staff and laying down how gaols were to be managed. It provided *inter alia* that no prisoner was to be put in irons except in case of necessity and that food and bedding had to be provided for prisoners without means. Gaols must be periodically lime washed and cleansed once a week; soap towel and comb must be provided; no liquor or gaming was to be allowed and trading with prisoners was prohibited. The justices were to execute the Act; visiting justices were to be appointed whose duty it would be to report their findings to Quarter Sessions. An amending Act of the following year provided that no prisoner was to be put on the treadmill before conviction and those committed for trial were to be supplied with food without being obliged to work. Also, travelling allowances were to be given to discharged prisoners.

In some counties the justices, slow to take up the new powers given by Parliament, were equally slow to implement the 1823 Act. Although York was by no means the worst (it had early instituted the segregation of male and female felons and had long had its own chaplain and surgeon),[31] it had, since at least the mid eighteenth century, been fighting a largely losing battle against overcrowding caused by the increasing volume of committals. Certainly, in the first quarter of the nineteenth century, conditions still left a great deal to be desired. When Elizabeth Fry and her brother John Joseph Gurney visited in 1818 they noted (as had Howard forty years before) that prisoners were loaded in irons and that some had no shirts to their backs.

In 1824, after the grand jury had presented the gaol as insufficient in classification, employment and accommodation, the county justices appointed a building committee empowered to make necessary improvements. Adjacent land was acquired and plans were drawn up for an extra prison for 90 felons and 200 debtors and in 1826 work began. Designed by the architect, Peter Frederick Robinson, the new prison was completed in 1835.[32] Situated immediately to the east of Clifford's Tower, and

---

[31] There had been a surgeon since 1736 (F Drake, *Eboracum,* W. Bowyer, London., 1736, p. 287)
[32] It cost together with the land £203,000 (*Victoria History of the Counties of England – The City of York,* ed. R. B Pugh, Oxford University Press, 1961, p. 526).

surrounded by a castellated perimeter wall,[33] it comprised a gatehouse, a house for the governor, and three blocks of cells radiating off a central spine.

While it was being built steps were taken by the magistrates to implement the new Gaol Act. By 1824 bedding, coals and soap were being provided by the county and chaining had been almost completely abandoned. Prisoners were also allowed access to books and by 1832 writing materials were available to would be learners.

When the new prison was finished, the offices were removed from the Female Prison to the gatehouse and the governor and most of the male felons to the new block.

From the very beginning one of its most serious deficiencies was the lack of work for prisoners. A prison inspector's report of 1848 complained of:

> 'unrestrained intercourse between prisoners, no special cells for solitary confinement and too many debtors living in comfort and treating the prison as 'a luxurious kind of poorhouse.'[34]

Eventually in 1858 workshops were built. When, in 1864, it was enacted that Leeds should henceforth be the Assize town for the West Riding, the result was an immediate downgrading of the Castle; it would now serve as the county gaol only for the East and North Ridings, both of which were principally agricultural in character and which, compared with the West Riding, generated relatively little serious crime. Sheffield prisoners sent for trial at Assizes would now be committed to and, if sentenced to death, hanged outside Armley prison.[35]

---

[33] The wall made of gritstone, which took years to build and proved very expensive, was known as Sydney Smith's hardest joke (the Rev Sydney Smith was one of the magistrates on the building committee): Alan Bell, *Sidney Smith,* Clarendon Press, Oxford, 1980, p. 111.

[34] Report, Inspector of Prisons (1848) [1055] (N & E. District, pp 24,26, 28 H.C. (1849), xxvi; in the report for 1856 it was stated that 'smoking appears to be the principal, if not the only, occupation of the debtors.'

[35] In 1900 the male prison was made available to the War Office as a military detention barracks, with the female prison retained for the confinement of suspects awaiting trial. In 1929 the military prison was closed. In 1932 the building ceased to be a prison at all. Two years later it was sold to York Corporation, which demolished it, opening the castle yard to the public.

Trial [36]

The coming of the Assize judges to York meant that for the remand prisoners in the Castle the wait was almost over. Within a week they would know whether they were to hang or go free. For the inns, eating houses and shopkeepers it meant an upsurge in business as jurors, witnesses and lawyers descended on the city. For the citizenry it was a time of pageant and excitement[37] which more often than not would culminate in a few hangings.

England was divided, for Assize purposes, into six circuits. Each Spring and Summer the twelve common law judges would leave London to take the Assizes,[38] two judges travelling each circuit, one to deliver the gaols (i.e. to try crime) the other to try civil causes. The counties within a circuit were visited in a fixed order, with a given number of days allotted to each Assize town. The largest circuit was the Northern which, until 1864, comprised Yorkshire, Lancashire, Durham, Northumberland, Cumberland and Westmoreland. In summer the judges visited York first, travelled next to Durham and then Newcastle and then west to Carlisle before turning south for Appleby and Lancaster. In Spring they did not visit the four northern counties the circuit starting at Lancaster and finishing at York. Only in 1820, after a two-year

---

[36] On the subject of trial procedure, see D. Bentley, *English Criminal Justice in the Nineteenth Century* (Hambledon, London, 1998).

[37] For the nobility and gentry of the county Assize week was one of the social occasions of the year. There would normally be an Assize Ball and usually other diversions such as an Assize concert and special productions at the Theatre Royal. See G Benson, *York from the Reformation to 1925* (Cooper and Swann, York, 1925), p 93 'Formerly the time of the Assizes was one of the fashionable seasons in York in which musical entertainments were prominent' and see also *York Gazette*, March 14, 1840:

> On Monday evening last, the usual Assize Ball was held in the ...Assembly Rooms at which about 200 of the nobility and gentry of the county of York and the neighbourhood attended... Tea and refreshments were provided by Mr Orton of the *Turf Tavern* and Hardman's Quadrille Band was stationed in the orchestra. Dancing was kept up by the majority of the assembly until a late hour.
>
> The first Assize Concert under the patronage of the High Sheriff took place on Tuesday evening in the Assembly Rooms. We are informed that the assembly of rank and fashion from all parts of the county on this occasion has never been exceeded on any first Assize Concert.
>
> A splendid entertainment on an extensive scale was given by the Lady Mayoress [at the Mansion House] on Wednesday evening last.

[38] Between 1822 and 1834 and again after 1843 a third (winter) criminal assize was held in populous counties such as Yorkshire.

campaign by the MP for Durham, were they given a Spring Assize. After Liverpool was made an Assize town in 1833 both circuits ended there.

In the eighteenth century Hull had its own Assize (held once every three years) but in 1794 it had been discontinued at the town's request, because of the expense of entertaining the judges. The city of York, like the town of Hull, was a county in its own right and it too had its own Assize which was held in the Guildhall at the same time as the Assize for the (geographical) county. The county Assizes were held at the Castle.[39] In the seventeenth century the building used had been the Moot Hall, which stood on the site now occupied by the former Female Prison. In 1777, however, a new court-house was built which is used today for Crown Court hearings.

The preparations for an Assize began several months before the judges left for the country. Which judges would travel which circuit was decided by ballot[40] and, once this had been settled, the Commission giving them authority to hold the Assizes would be drawn up and signed by the King. The decision as to the number of sitting days to be allotted to each county was taken once the lists of prisoners for trial had been received from the sheriffs.

Until the advent of the railways it was customary for the judges to arrive in York by carriage (usually on a Saturday). As their carriage approached the city it would be met by the high sheriff of the county,[41] accompanied by his friends and by javelin men, who would escort them the rest of the way to the ringing of church bells and the sounding of

---

[39] Courts had been held at the castle since at least the thirteenth century. 'There were six periods when the [King's Bench, Common Pleas] and the Exchequer were in York although the three courts did not always remain together throughout the whole of them: 1298-1304, 1319-20, 1322-23, 1327-28, 1333-37 and 1392. Rooms in the castle were first set aside for the Exchequer and Common Pleas in 1298. ...Judging from the terms used in documents of the late fourteenth century the Common Plcas sat in thc Great Hall of the Castle and the King's Bench and Exchequer in the Little Hall: *Victoria History of the Counties of England,, The City of York*, (ed R.B Pugh) Oxford University Press, 1961, p. 522.

[40] A judge could not travel a circuit from which he haled or in which he had property without special royal dispensation: J S Cockburn, *A History of English Assizes, 1558-1714* (Cambridge University Press, 1972), p. 49.

[41] If travelling from the south the judges would be met at Holgate; if coming from Durham at Dring-houses (see e.g. *York Gazette*, March 7, 1840).

trumpets.[42] They would go first to the Castle and to the Guildhall for the reading of the Commission and then to their lodgings.[43] The following day they would attend Divine Service in the Minster. On March 16 1822 the *York Herald* described thus the ceremony with which the Lent Assizes had been opened on the previous Saturday:

> On Saturday last the sheriffs of the county and city, with a large cavalcade of tenantry and friends, met Mr. Justice Holroyd at Holgate and accompanied his lordship into this city where he arrived between 7 and 8 o'clock in the evening and immediately proceeded to the Castle and to the Guildhall where he opened the Commission of Assize for the county and the city of York. The procession into the city would have been extremely splendid had it been aided by favourable weather and earlier arrival of the judge, for beside the usual equipage and additional attendances of the High Sheriff of the County, the city Sheriffs and their two chaplains appeared in two coaches and four, followed by a very respectable retinue of friends of each, of the numerous tenantry of Mr Sheriff Stapylton from the Myton estate and from his several other estates in this county of York. On Sunday morning Mr Justice Holroyd attended divine worship at the Cathedral. The usual procession was preceded by about 100 of the tenantry of Mr Bethell who walked arm in arm ... until they came near the Cathedral steps where they opened right and left and the procession passed through their ranks; they then formed again and followed the procession into the Church where an appropriate discourse was delivered by the Rev. Henry Torre, the High Sheriff's Chaplain from the Eighth Chapter of Hebrews, 10th verse.
>
> Mr. Justice Bayley entered the city privately on Sunday.[44]

---

[42] Surtees Society, Vol 40, *York Castle Depositions* (Frances Andrews, Durham, 1861), viii 'The journey of the dispensers of the law in many respects resembled the progresses of royalty.' The procession to meet the judges involved the county sheriff in considerable expense. He had to pay for the coachman, postilion, footman, trumpeters and halberdmen (in the eighteenth century each was paid 2/6 per day and a further sum for horse hire) and for their liveries. It was also usual for him to provide a dinner for those of his tenantry who accompanied him to meet the judges. In 1840 the *York Gazette* for March 14 reported that 'subsequent to the return of the procession...upwards of 70 of the High Sheriff's tenantry sat down to an excellent dinner provided for them at the expense of that gentleman.' But all this was only part of the expense of the office. It was customary for the sheriff to provide a dinner at his Inn on Commission Day and to entertain the grand jury to dinner on Monday in the first Assize week and there were a hundred and one other disbursements to be made. Tradesmen's bills normally came to about £850 with a further £800 disbursed in other ways (see generally G Benson, *York from Reformation to 1925,* pp 130-31).

[43] The judge's lodgings were originally in Spurriergate but were later in Coney Street opposite the *George Inn.* In 1806 in order to provide the judges with more convenient accommodation a doctor's house in Lendal was purchased by the city magistrates. This building is today a hotel called *The Judge's Lodgings.* 'The allowance provided for the lodgings at each Assize used to be four hogsheads of beer, 3 chalders of coals and 3000 turves and charcoal. The beds were to be aired for a week before the Assize' (Ronald Willis, *A Portrait of York* (3rd edn, Robert Hale, London, 1982), p. 92).

[44] Cf *Hull Rockingham,* March 29 1834, Yorkshire Lent Assizes:

> These Assizes for the county of York and the city and county of the same were opened on Saturday last with the accustomed formalities. In the forenoon Henry Preston Esq the High Sheriff arrived at Baker's Lodgings in Blake St and was greeted with a peel on the Cathedral bells and those of St Martin's, Coney St. In the afternoon the usual cavalcade set out to meet the judges.
>
> The liveries which were furnished by Messrs Strickland were very handsome. The servants and trumpeters wearing white, faced with crimson and richly trimmed with silver lace, and the halberdmen having uniforms of crimson faced with white.
>
> Before the procession reached Holgate the travelling carriage of Sir W E Taunton, one of the judges, had arrived at that village and the cavalcade which extended nearly a mile in length

At the Summer Assize 1841 the judges arrived in York by train – the first time they had done so.[45] Thereafter they invariably travelled to the city by train, being met at the railway station by the two sheriffs with the usual cavalcade of tenantry, trumpeters, halberdiers and footmen in attendance.[46]

On the Monday following the Assize service the work of the Assize would begin. After breakfasting with the Lord Mayor at the Mansion House the judges would separate, one proceeding to the Guildhall the other to the Castle, their arrival announced by a fanfare of trumpets. At the Guildhall the criminal list would be taken first followed by any civil pleas; once the work was finished (and it rarely took long) the judge would move to the Castle where he would make a start on the county civil list. By this time his brother judge would already have got under way with the trial of

---

reformed and returned to the city. The whole then proceeded to the Castle where the Commission of Assize was opened with the usual formalities and the court was adjourned to 12 o'clock on Monday.

On leaving the castle the city sheriff's carriage and four was waiting in Tower Street into which the learned judge was received by Mr Sheriff Coates and Mr Sheriff Hotham and he immediately proceeded to the Guildhall where the Commission of Assize for the city of York and the county of the same city was opened in due form and the court was adjourned to Monday morning at 9 o'clock. Mr Justice Alderson arrived privately in the evening. Sunday morning there was a very full attendance at the Cathedral and at the door of the choir being thrown open at a quarter past 10 o'clock every seat except those kept for official personages was immediately filled. At a quarter before 11 the corporate body in their state robes entered the Minster by the grand west entrance and were followed by the judges and the High Sheriff. They were met in the aisle by the dignitaries, the clergy and the choristers preceded by the verger.

Divine service was commenced (Sermon, 1 Cor xiv, 1 'Follow after Charity'). The afternoon service was also numerously attended many strangers being present Sir E H Alderson was present on this occasion but without the paraphernalia of official office.

[45] *York Gazette*, July 17, 1841.
[46] *York Gazette*, July 17, 1847: Saturday July 10:

The York Summer Assizes commenced at York this day. The arrival of Joseph Dent Esq., High Sheriff of the county at his official residence in this city was announced by a peal from the Cathedral bells at about noon. At three in the afternoon he proceeded in state to meet the learned judges, the Lord Chief Baron and Mr Justice Wightman, who were expected from town by the express train which reaches York at half past three. The High Sheriff was accompanied by his chaplain in the State carriage, which was followed by Mrs. Dent's private carriage and the carriage of the High Sheriff of the City. The usual cavalcade of halbardiers, footmen, etc. was in attendance and the procession was headed by a large number of Mr Dent's tenantry. On the arrival of the train it was found that only one of the learned judges had come viz. Mr Justice Wightman, the Lord Chief Baron being engaged in trying *Nisi Prius* cases at Guildhall, London. After his lordship was robed he was conducted to the castle.

The judges were still being met off the train by a sheriffs' cavalcade as late as 1864: *York Gazette*, March 26, 1864.

the county criminal work. At both venues the first important task was the swearing and charging of the grand jury.

The grand jury was a filter whose purpose was to weed out weak and baseless cases. Only a grand jury could find a bill of indictment[47] against an accused and a prosecutor seeking an indictment had to lay his evidence before it for its scrutiny. It consisted of not less than twelve nor more than twenty-three jurors and reached its decision by majority vote. Assize grand juries were drawn in the main from the county magistracy. In his charge to them the judge would draw their attention to that state of crime in the county and give them legal directions about any case likely to give cause difficulty. Following this the jury would retire to their room. The witnesses in the various cases would then be sworn in open court and sent along to the grand jury room to wait their turn to be examined by the jury. The examination would be conducted in private and in the accused's absence. If in a case the jury were satisfied that there was *prima facie* evidence of guilt they would endorse the proposed indictment 'true bill' and it would be carried into court to be tried; if they were not so satisfied, they would endorse it ' *ignoramus'* [48] or 'no true bill,' in which event the accused would, at the end of the Assize be discharged 'by proclamation' (which would usually be an end to the prosecution).

As soon as indictments began to emerge for the grand jury room,[49] the court would begin to try them. An accused against whom an indictment had been found would be arraigned on it, that is called into the dock and asked to plead to it. If his plea was not guilty, a jury would be sworn to try him. If, however, he wilfully refused to plead or to agree to be tried, he would be put to the *peine forte et dure*, that is he would be taken to the press-yard, spread-eagled on the ground and loaded with weights until he either

---

[47] An indictment was, and still is, a written accusation of one of more persons of crime at the suit of the King (Queen).

[48] I.e. we know nothing of it.

[49] At York (as a safeguard against tampering) indictments found by the grand jury were placed in a locked wooden box (known as the grand jury letter box) which was lowered to the court floor from the magistrates' gallery by means of a rod passed through the handle (at some courts a fishing net was used).

consented to be tried or expired.[50] In 1772 the *peine forte et dure* was abolished; henceforth a wilful refusal to plead or to agree to jury trial would be treated as equivalent to a plea of guilty. This remained the law until 1827 when it was enacted that in such cases the court should simply direct that a plea of not guilty be entered.

The jury who would try the accused would be all-male. It would be chosen by ballot from the jurors summoned by the sheriff, with the accused having the right to challenge up to twenty jurors without cause and an unlimited number for cause shown. Most Assize juries consisted of shopkeepers and small farmers.

The accused was required to stand not just when the jury was being empanelled but during the whole of the trial. Only if he was infirm, would he be allowed to sit.

Once the jury had been sworn, prosecuting counsel, if there was one, would open (outline) the Crown case to them and then call his witnesses. If, however, the prosecutor had not retained counsel (and in the eighteenth and early nineteenth centuries many did not), the judge would prosecute, calling the witnesses in turn and examining them from the depositions they had made before the committing magistrates.

The common law did not permit those accused of felony to have counsel to defend them (a rule defended by Chief Justice Coke on the ground that, where a man was on trial for his life, the law required that the evidence to convict [him] should be so manifest that it could not be contradicted). By the mid eighteenth century, however, it had become usual to allow the accused to have counsel to question witnesses on his behalf. Such counsel was not, however, permitted to address the jury; this the prisoner had to do for himself. Not until 1836 was the law on this point altered.

If the accused could not afford to pay counsel, and most could not, he had to defend himself. Trials of undefended prisoners were usually quick and hopelessly one-sided, their efforts at defence being generally 'pitiable even if [they had] a good case.'[51] In the 1820s some judges began to adopt the practice of asking counsel present in court to undertake the defence of undefended prisoners. The request, which was never refused,

---

[50]   Wm Andrews, *Bygone Punishments*, 2nd edn 1931, p 80 '[he shall be] laid on his back and as many weights shall be laid upon him as he can bear and more.'

[51]   J .F. Stephen, *A History of the Criminal Law of England* (MacMillan & Co., London, 1883), i, p 442.

was normally only made in cases in which the prisoner was likely to be left for execution if convicted.[52] By 1850 it had become usual for counsel to be assigned where the charge was murder. Also, at the insistence of the judges, Assize prosecutions were by now always prosecuted by counsel.

After the prosecution had closed its case, the accused had the right to call defence witnesses. He was not, however, permitted to give evidence himself nor might his wife be a witness for him. Lawyers offered two justifications for the rule; first, since he was personally interested in the outcome of the case, any evidence which he or his wife gave was likely to be biased and perjured; second, the rule protected him against self-incrimination; to abolish it would lead to the establishment of something akin to the disliked French form of procedure with prisoners compelled by rigorous cross-examination (conducted where there was no prosecuting counsel by the judge) to convict themselves out of their own mouths. The accused was, however, entitled to make an unsworn statement from the dock (upon which he could not be questioned) explaining, as best he could, his answer to the charge and attempting to point out the deficiencies in the prosecution case (although, after 1836, even this right was denied to him if he was defended by counsel, on the ground that a prisoner could not have counsel speak for him and address the jury himself).[53] Most poor prisoners had the greatest difficulty in getting witnesses to court, particularly where they came from a place distant from the Assize town.

After the defence case had closed the judge would sum the case up to the jury, telling them the law they needed to know to try it and reminding them of the evidence called. The jury would then consider their verdict, which had to be unanimous. Where the case was clear the jury would not even trouble to leave the jury box, delivering their verdict after a brief whispered discussion. They could, however, if they wished, retire to their jury room to deliberate. Once they had retired they would be denied food, drink and fire until they had brought back a verdict. If they had not reached a verdict by the time the judge was ready to leave for the next Assize town, it was open to him to have

---

[52] Of the Sheffield hanged whose stories are given hereafter we know of eleven (Lastley, Stevens, Bennet, Broughton, Slack, Allott, Williams, Nall, Waddington, Barbour and Myers) who were defended by counsel.

[53] See generally D. Bentley, op. cit., chapters 15 and 17.

them put in a cart; the cart would travel behind him and, if they had still not agreed by the time he reached the county border, they would be shot into a ditch. In Parliamentary debates in the 1860s the Law lords were at pains to assert that carting had never been practised or sanctioned by the common law. This was, however, untrue. An Irish jury was carted at Tralee Assizes in 1825 while, as late as 1848, Baron Platt when sitting at Oxford Assizes, gave orders for a cart to be got ready for a jury which could not agree.

Because juries in felony cases were forbidden to separate once the trial had begun, it was common for courts to sit late into the evening to spare them the hardship of being locked up in the court-house overnight or over the weekend.[54] At busy assizes courts also sat late in order to get through the calendar of work.

If the verdict was not guilty, the prisoner would be discharged and left to make his own way back to his home-town, on foot if need be. For those from the south of the county this meant a long walk. When John Booth was acquitted of robbery at the 1790 Lent Assizes lack of money obliged him to walk back to Sheffield, which he reached two days later.

Prisoners found guilty, or who had pleaded guilty on arraignment, were in the eighteenth century often sentenced in batches at the end of the Assize. Those convicted of felony would before sentence be asked it they had anything to say why sentence should not be passed upon them.[55] The purpose of the question was to enable to prisoners to raise any matter which might operate as a bar to their being sentenced or afford grounds for postponement of sentence. Until 1825, in the case of the lesser felonies, one such matter was benefit of clergy (by 1800 this amounted in effect to a plea that the accused had not previously been convicted of felony) which would result in the prisoner being imprisoned instead of hanged. Another was pregnancy, which, if established to the satisfaction of a jury of matrons, would result in a female felon having her execution put off until she had born the child she was carrying (only after 1840 would pregnancy operate to secure a permanent reprieve). Those capitally convicted who had no motion available to them would be sentenced to death.

---

[54] Hence Pope's lines, *The Rape of the Lock*, canto 3, 21
    'The hungry judges soon the sentence sign,
    And wretches hang that jurymen may dine.'
[55] *Allocutus* was the technical name for this demand or question.

The form of death sentence varied according to the nature of the offence. For felony the penalty was hanging. Treason however attracted an aggravated penalty: hanging drawing and quartering in the case of male traitors, burning for women. Also, by the Murder Act 1751 a judge passing sentence on a murderer was obliged to direct that after execution his body either be gibbeted (hung in chains)[56] near to the scene of his crime, or handed over to surgeons for dissection.[57] In 1746 twenty-four Jacobites who had taken part in Bonnie Prince Charlie's rebellion were tried at York, hung drawn and quartered on the Knavesmire and the heads of two of them placed on spikes on Micklegate Bar. This horrific mode of execution (last employed in 1820) remained part of English law until 1870. In the eighteenth century three women were burned at York for the *petit treason* of murdering their husbands.[58] In 1790, however, Parliament substituted hanging as the punishment for female traitors. In 1832 the power to direct that murderers' bodies be handed over for dissection was abolished, a reform which deprived medical schools of a source of anatomical specimens. Gibbeting was put an end to in 1834.

Not all of those sentenced to death would, however, be executed. It was open to the trial judge to recommend that a convicted felon be pardoned on condition of undergoing some lesser penalty such as transportation. Such recommendations contained in a circuit letter despatched by the judge at the end of the Assize were

---

[56] At Newgate a body which was to be gibbeted was taken to a place called 'the Kitchen' where stood a cauldron of boiling pitch. Into this the corpse was thrown and then shortly after pulled out, placed in chains and cold riveted into the metal frame in which it would be suspended from the gibbet: J. Laurence, *A History of Capital Punishment*, Sampson Low, London, p. 59. Whether the same procedure was followed at York is not known.

[57] Dissection was greatly feared by the poor. The reason is well explained by Ian Rankin, *The Falls* (Orion, London, 2001), p. 80 '...a dissected body cannot rise up on the day of judgment' The bodies of York criminals ordered for dissection were usually taken to the York County Hospital but not always. In March 1809 the body of Mary Bateman, hanged for poisoning, was taken for dissection to the Leeds General Infirmary where the hospital authorities decided to charge visitors 3d to view the body (a proceeding which left the hospital £30 the richer) (Knipe, *Criminal Chronology of York Castle* (C L Burdekin, York, 1867), p. 149).

[58] The mode of execution is described by Twyford & Griffiths, op. cit., p 49: the condemned woman would be chained to a stake near the gallows and a fire built and lit; before the flames reached her she would be strangled 'by means of a rope passed around the neck and pulled by the executioner so that she was dead before the flames reached her body.' When Catherine Hayes was executed at the London Tyburn in 1726 the executioner's attempt to strangle her failed and the horrified crowd watched her burnt alive. Three women were burnt at York in the eighteenth century: Mary Ellah (March 30, 1757); Ann Sowerby (August 10, 1767) and Eliza Bordington (March 29, 1776); according to Knipe, Ellah and Bordington were hanged and Sowerby strangled before being burnt.

always acted upon. Before leaving an Assize town the judge would inform the sheriff which of the prisoners under sentence of death he was recommending for pardon and which were left for execution. In 1824, so that prisoners whom the judge intended to spare might be saved the ordeal of hearing sentence of death pronounced, Parliament enacted that in such cases the judge might simply direct that sentence of death be recorded. In the main, those recommended for pardon were prisoners convicted of one of the less serious felonies who were of good character or who had other substantial mitigation. Those convicted of murder, rape or robbery were rarely, if ever, spared.

Against conviction for felony there was no right of appeal. If the trial judge felt doubt about some point of law which had arisen during the trial, it was open to him to refer the point to his fellow judges and to postpone execution until their opinion was known, but it was entirely in his discretion whether he did so and very few cases were in fact reserved. It was always open to the accused's friends or lawyers to petition the Crown that his life be spared. If they could lay before the Home Office new evidence or other compelling grounds for intervention success was possible, although in the case of prisoners convicted in towns such as York, far distant from London, their main battle would be against the clock: in an age when the horse was the fastest means of travel and there was neither telegraph nor telephone, it was not unknown for reprieves to arrive after the subject had been executed. In April 1776 the execution of James Proctor was delayed two hours beyond the usual time because hopes of a reprieve were entertained.

After receiving sentence of death, a prisoner would be placed in one of the condemned cells of the Castle Prison. He would be ministered to by the prison Chaplain who would seek to bring him to a state of repentance and grace. A condemned sermon would be preached in the prison chapel and there would also be an opportunity for the prisoner to take his leave of friends and family either face to face or in a letter. Not all were prepared to submit meekly to their fate. In 1764 Charles Dorrington, in order to gain a few more hours of life, barricaded himself in his cell on the morning he was due to hang; 'Life is sweet' he explained to the turnkeys when they eventually broke down the cell door. In 1785 Robert Crosby and John Edwards under sentence of death for arson broke out of the Castle never to be recaptured. Others tried to cheat the hangman by taking their own lives. In 1759 Eugene Aram was found with his wrists cut and bleeding but quickly patched up and hurried off to the scaffold. In 1775 Captain John Bolton hanged himself in his cell rather than suffer a shameful death on the gallows.

Execution

In the eighteenth century, prisoners left for execution were normally hanged within days of the judges departing the city. Those convicted of murder were executed on the second day after sentence passed,[59] others usually on the Saturday following the end of the Assize.[60] In 1836, however, the statutory provision requiring murderers to be executed within 48 hours of sentence was repealed and shortly afterwards the government announced that henceforth an interval of 14 to 27 days between sentence and execution would be allowed in all capital cases.[61] That Saturday should have been the favoured day for hanging is hardly surprising, for then the city would be thronged with people thereby maximising the deterrent effect.

In the seventeenth century there were two gallows at York. Both stood outside the city walls and were used for the execution of city and county malefactors alike. One, named Tyburn, after its London counterpart, was on the Knavesmire [62] close by the Tadcaster Road.[63]

---

[59] Unless that day was a Sunday in which case it would take place on the Monday following - Murder Act, 1751, s. 3.

[60] Occasionally executions had to be respited, as where a female felon was declared by a jury of matrons to be with child or when the judge wished to take the opinion of his brethren about the case.

[61] It was repealed by 6 & 7 Will. 4, c. 30 as a precaution against a possible execution of offenders convicted upon erroneous evidence.

[62] Twyford and Griffiths, op. cit, p 92. The London Tyburn took its name from the river Tyburn which, near the gallows site, ran in two streams or burns (two burns).

[63] Opposite Hob Moor Lane. Today its site is marked by a stone inscribed with the word Tyburn which stands on a stone platform at the side of the A1036 approximately ¾ mile south of Micklegate Bar opposite Pulleyn Drive. When I first visited on April 18, 2001 a bunch of flowers had been left there, attached to which was a card which read 'In memory of Samuel Lundy hanged at York 1801' (Lundy who came from Market Weighton was executed on April 11, 1801 for cow stealing). A gallows was first

The other at St Leonard's, Green Dykes on the Hull road.[64] The St Leonard's Gallows fell out of use in the last quarter of the century [65] and at the Lent Assize 1700 the grand jury presented a petition to the judges for its removal. On June 1 the county sheriff received an order from the Home Office for it to be taken down. Two days later it was demolished leaving Tyburn as the sole place of execution for both county and city felons.

On the day fixed for an execution, a horse-drawn cart [66] would be brought to the entrance of the Castle prison and the under-sheriff would demand the body of the prisoner. Inside the prison the condemned would be brought from his cell to the unshackling yard where his fetters would be struck off.[67] He would then be taken out to the cart.[68] Once its escort of sheriff's men and dragoons was in place, the cart would set off, followed by a group of officials including the governor of the castle and the under-sheriff. The chaplain would commonly ride in the cart with the condemned, reading the burial service as he went. It would emerge from the castle yard into Castle Gate, watched by a large crowd many of whom would swarm around, intent on following it to Tyburn. At the top of Castle Gate, it would turn onto the Ouse Bridge and begin the

---

erected at Tyburn in March 1379; it was built by Master Joseph Penny of Blake Street; the cost was £10.15.0.

[64]   The gallows stood on Garrow Hill (thought to be a corruption of Gallows Hill). A nearby road used by the execution cart is still known as Thief Lane. The editors of the volume *The City of York* in the *Victoria County History* observe at p 257 that 'the land in Green Dykes was in the possession of the Hospital of St Leonard and the master of that great secular institution no doubt claimed the privilege of *infangthief* (the power to hang thieves caught red handed on his lands) and the right of gallows;' they add at pp. 496-97 that the gallows is recorded as in use from 1374-75 until 1444-45, out of use in 1550 but back in use in 1571 and thereafter often used until 1676.

[65]   It had last been used on May 1, 1676 for the execution of two sheep stealers Leonard Gaskill and Peter Rook.

[66]   In the eighteenth century felons of rank were occasionally driven to the place of execution in their own carriages. In 1760 Earl Ferrers, hanged for the murder of his steward, rode to Tyburn in his own coach. The year before William Andrew Horne, who was hanged on his 74th birthday, was driven to Gallows Hill, Nottingham by his own coachman; according to W. Andrews, *Bygone Punishments* (2nd edn., 1931) p. 15: 'as the gloomy procession ascended the Mansfield Road the white locks of the hoary sinner streamed mournfully in the wind.' It would seem that in 1781 the privilege was granted to William Meyers, a Yorkshire criminal, hanged at York Tyburn for murder; Knipe, op. cit., p 91, describes him as being taken to Tyburn in a mourning coach, with a hearse attending to bring back his body and being put onto the cart at the gallows.

[67]   According to Hargrove, *History and Description of the Ancient City of York* (William Alexander, York, 1818), p 880 the unshackling was carried out in the exercise yard at the side of the Debtors' Prison (known as half moon yard).

[68]   The cart would contain his coffin; when there were several convicts to hang they would travel in one cart which would be followed by a second containing their coffins cf Knipe, op. cit., pp 110, 134.

climb up Micklegate. Through Micklegate Bar it would go and out along the Tadcaster road. At Tyburn there would be more people waiting. Often the crush was so great that the cart would have to halt repeatedly along the route so that a way could be cleared for it. When a batch of fifteen prisoners was hanged in 1649 it took the carts carrying them just under an hour to travel the mile and a half from the Castle to the gallows.[69]

In London, in the eighteenth century, it was customary for the cart to stop along its route (usually at St Giles) to allow the prisoner to take ale.[70] Did York have a similar tradition? Possibly.[71] At least one occasion is known when the cart was stopped and wine sent for from a nearby ale house[72] and legend has it that the life of a Bawtry saddler would have been saved if he had taken the liquor offered to him along the route (according to tradition a reprieve was on its way and, had he stopped to take the customary bowl of ale, it would have arrived in time to save his life).[73]

The York Tyburn, like its London namesake, was a triple tree (i.e. it consisted of three cross beams arranged in a triangle supported at each corner by a wooden post).[74]

---

[69] Cf Knipe, op. cit., p 29 'On entering Castlegate that street appeared one mass of human beings and the solemn procession was stopped for some time before it could proceed the people were so closely jammed together. They were stopped several times in Micklegate by reason of the great number of spectators that thronged the road. When the Merringtons were executed at St Leonard's in the same year (see n 72 below) the crush in Fossgate was so great that two spectators suffered broken legs: Knipe, op. cit., p. 26)

[70] Cf Swift's poem *Clever Tom Clinch, Going to be Hanged* (1727).

> As clever Tom Clinch, while the rabble was bawling
> Rode stately through Holborn to die of his Calling
> He stopt at the George for a bottle of sack
> And promised to pay for it when he came back.'

[71] Any such halt would probably have been in Micklegate where there was no shortage of hostelries (e,g, *The Falcon, The Nag's Head* (Alan Johnson, *The Inns and Alehouses of York* (Hutton Press, Beverley, 1980).

[72] In 1649 when George and Maria Merrington were being taken for execution at St Leonard's, the crush of people in Walmgate was so great that both fainted; the sheriff ordered the proprietress of the nearby *Golden Barrel* to give them some mint water and after their recovery each had a glass of wine' Knipe, op. cit., p 26.

[73] The story is told in W. Andrews, op. cit., p.11 and is cited by Radzinowicz, op. cit., vol. 1, p 173. It appears to be apocryphal. According to Knipe the only Bawtry man executed at the York Tyburn was Robert Dyson hanged in August 1797 for embezzlement. He was not a saddler and the account of his execution makes no mention of any reprieve.

[74] It went by the nickname 'The three-legged Mare of York.'

Ladder hanging - The print depicts 'Half-hanged Smith' (as to whom see chapter 5) being taken down from the gallows. The ladder from which he was turned off minutes before is clearly visible.

Cart hanging - This print was often used by publishers of broadsheets. (see e.g. the Charlesworth broadsheet p.88)

The 'Three-legged Mare of York'
An eighteenth-century pencil drawing of the Tyburn gallows.

The Tyburn Platform - The paved platform (which is of recent construction)
today serves to indicate the approximate location of the Tyburn gallows.
It lies across from and a few yards to the south of Pulleyn Road.

The Tyburn Stone - A close-up of the commemorative marker stone on the platform.

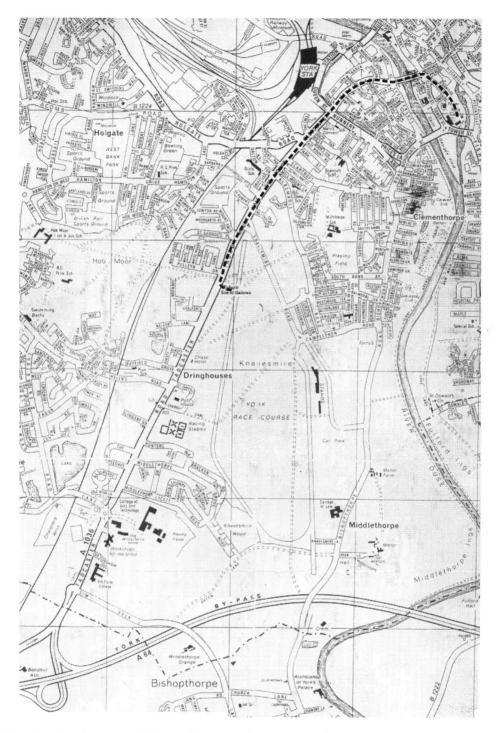

Map showing the route to Tyburn. The execution cart started its journey outside the goal and travelled along Castlegate, over the Ouse Bridge, along Micklegate, through Micklegate Bar and along the Tadcaster Road to Tyburn.

View of Castlegate along which the execution cart would pass at the start of its journey.

View of the Ouse Bridge and Micklegate along which the cart would pass
as it climbed to Micklegate Bar.

GREEN DYKES LN.

THIEF LANE

GARROW HILL

Present day York streets with links to the gallows at St Leonard's, Green Dykes.

Garrow is thought to be a corruption of gallows.

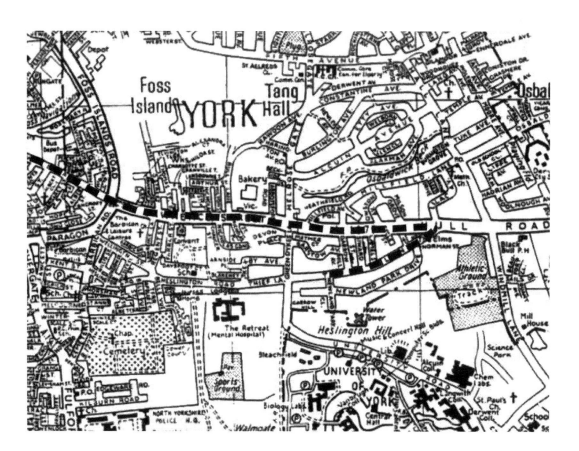

Map showing the conjectured route from the Castle to the St Leonard's gallows.

Until the mid-eighteenth century the practice was for the hangman to use a ladder which he would place against one of the cross-beams. He would then ascend it leading the condemned by a rope which he had put around his neck; the rope was then attached to the beam and the prisoner turned off the ladder.[75] By 1760, however, the method had changed: the cart was now drawn up beneath the beam and the prisoner made to stand up; the noose was placed around his neck and, upon a signal given by the executioner, the horse would be given a touch of the whip and would draw away leaving the condemned man suspended from the beam. Death was not instantaneous. The drop being too short to break his neck the prisoner would be slowly strangled.[76] To cut short his agonies the hangman or the man's friends would sometimes pull on his legs. Before being turned off, the prisoner would normally be allowed time for prayer, often all the while being exhorted by the chaplain to confess his guilt.[77] Usually he would be permitted a last speech thereby providing copy for pamphleteers. Meyers executed in 1781 spent 70 minutes talking to the sheriff and addressing the crowd before finally being turned off.

In the eighteenth century after the body had been cut down it would, unless the judge had ordered that it be gibbeted or dissected, be handed over to friends or family for burial. After 1836, however, the bodies of murderers were by statute required to be buried within the precincts of the prison.[78]

---

[75] This was the way in which Turpin was hanged cf *York Courant*, April 10th 1739: 'it was very remarkable that as he mounted the ladder his right leg trembled on which he stampt it down ... and with undoubted courage looked round about him and after speaking a few words to the Topsman he threw himself off the ladder and expired in about five minutes.' Cf the account of the execution of Colonel James Turner at Tyburn in 1663 given by J. Atholl, *Shadow of the Gallows* (John Long, London, 1954), p 67: 'on feeling the rope pull somewhat as he mounted the ladder, [he] turned on the executioner and demanded, "Dost thou intend to choke me? Pray, fellow give me more rope! How long have you been an executioner that you know not where to put the knot."

[76] Occasionally the hangman did not even manage to kill his victim. In 1280 an executed criminal on being taken from the Knavesmire to nearby St James chapel for burial was found to be alive (*Victoria History of the Counties of England, The City of York*, p. 376). A similar incident occurred in 1634. On March 27 John Bartendale was executed at Tyburn for felony. After hanging for three-quarters of an hour he was cut down and buried near the gallows. Shortly after a passer-by saw the earth heaving and with the help of a servant 'dug the convict up alive.' Barterndale was taken back to the Castle and eventually pardoned (Twyford & Griffith, op. cit., pp 110-11).

[77] According to a report in the *York Courant* for April 10, 1739 Turpin shortly before he was turned off declared himself to be the notorious highwayman Turpin and confessed to the executioner a great number of robberies which he had committed.

[78] The statute 2 & 3 Wm IV (1832) c. 75, s 16 which repealed the power to order dissection required the judge to direct either that the body of a murderer either be gibbeted or buried within the precincts of the

The long journey to Tyburn was an ordeal with which prisoners coped in different ways. Some, dressed in shrouds, spent the time left to them praying.[79] Some wore mourning or dressed as a bridegroom;[80] others sported a white cockade or feather as a mark of innocence. When Turpin, the highwayman, went to his death on a summer's day in 1739, he stood in the cart, dressed in a coat and pumps purchased specially for the occasion, bowing gravely to the crowd.[81] To men such as he what was important was to die and to be seen to die 'game.' [82] Although most condemned were resigned to their fate this was not true of all. In 1803 the convict Terry actually fought with the hangman on the scaffold.[83] Yet others took refuge in jest; as William Barwick was waiting for the noose to be placed around his neck he expressed the hope that the rope was strong enough to bear his weight, adding that if it broke and he was thrown to the ground he 'might be a cripple for life.'[84]

In London in 1783 the City authorities, in the interests of decency and public order, decided that henceforth executions would take place not at Tyburn but outside Newgate, using a temporary portable drop. In 1801 the authorities in York followed London's example. At a meeting of the county magistrates on July 23 it was resolved that henceforth executions should take place on a mound at the south-west end of the Assize Court, behind the Grand Jury room and facing the New Walk and St George's

---

prison in which he had been confined after conviction; the statute 4 & 5 Wm IV (1836) , c 21 abolished the power to order dissection, leaving burial within the prison as the disposal which the judge was required to order.

[79] According to a report in the *York Gazette*, August 7, 1841 it was usual on the eve of execution for condemned prisoners to sit up all night 'engaged in devotional exercises.'

[80] Cf M. Misson, *Memoirs and Observations in his Travels over England* (1719), p 124 'he that is to be hanged first takes care to get himself shaved and handsomely drest either in Mourning or in the Dress of a Bridgeroom.'

[81] Turpin also hired five poor men at 10s each to follow the cart as mourners: Knipe, op. cit, pp. 58-59.

[82] Cf Swift, *Clever Tom Clinch Going to be Hanged*:

> His waistcoat, and stockings and breeches were white;
> His cap had a new cherry ribbon to tie't.
> The maids to the doors and the balconies ran,
> And said 'Lack-a-day, he's a proper young man!
> But, as from the windows the ladies he spied,
> Like a beau in the box, he bow'd low on each side!

[83] Atholl, op. cit., p 77.

[84] Atholl, op. cit. p 67.

Field.[85] As at Newgate, a portable drop would be used which would be taken down after the hanging. The person principally instrumental in effecting this change had been Major Topham, one of the county magistrates. He had been campaigning for reform for over seven years, arguing that executions at Tyburn caused severe disruption to traffic and commerce, as well as offending the sensibilities of the humane and subjecting the condemned to an unnecessary ordeal,[86]

The last execution at Tyburn was that of Edward Hughes on August 29, 1801.[87] By August 1802 the new drop, built by Joseph Halfpenny, a local joiner, was ready. It was first used on the 18th of that month for the execution of Robert Barker and William Jackson. The drop, the trap of which was operated by ropes, was no more efficient as a killing machine than the old triple tree. Those hanged on it still strangled.[88]

The removal of the gallows to the Castle did not abate public enthusiasm for the spectacle.

> 'St George's Field was always crowded at executions. Such events were treated in the city as a 'gale day' and the factories and workshops closed for a short time so that the workmen might be at liberty to attend.'

Nor did the spectators come from just the city.

> 'York hangings drew crowds from far and near. At such time all the roads to York were thronged. After the railway was opened many came by train and on one occasion in 1856 ... it was lamented that no cheap excursions were run.' [89]

In the eighteenth century, after hangings, mock executions were frequently carried out in public house yards by the hangman and others hired by the inn-keepers.[90] There

---

[85] *York Herald*, July 25, 1801.

[86] A letter on the subject dated 10 July 1793 addressed to The High Sheriff of the county, the grand jury and his fellow county magistrates was published in the *York Courant*, July 15, 1793.

[87] It was finally dismantled in April 1812.

[88] In 1828, in order to give himself a longer drop and avoid being strangled, John Dyon 'stooped down to half his normal height so that the hangman had to lengthen the rope. He then stood up with the result that he had a fall of some feet' (Atholl, op. cit., p 111). Edward Wells hanged at Tyburn on April 28, 1753 is described as throwing himself off the cart with the greatest resolution as it was drawn away (Knipe, op. cit., p 63). John M'Naughten tried a violent jump at Strabane in 1761, but the rope broke, after which he had to wait until a man hanged with him was dead, so that the rope used to hang the latter could be re-used (Atholl, ibid).

[89] G. Benson, *York from Reformation to 1925*, p 91.

[90] T. P Cooper, op. cit., 1911, p 264.

was also a brisk trade, which carried on well into the following century, in pamphlets carrying accounts of the crimes and purported dying speeches of those executed.[91]

In many of the southern counties it was customary for the sheriff to employ the Newgate hangman. Yorkshire, however, had traditionally used a local hangman recruited, as often as not, from the ranks of condemned criminals.[92] For most of the first half of the nineteenth century the executioner was a Thirsk convict called John Curry. Sentenced to death for sheep stealing in March 1801 Curry had been pardoned on condition that he be transported for 14 years.[93] However, he never was transported. Instead he was imprisoned in the Castle for the whole of the 14-year term, acting when called upon as its executioner and continuing to do so after his release in 1815. He finally retired in 1835 and died six years later in the workhouse at Thirsk. His place was taken by James Coates, a Leeds man sentenced to transportation at the 1835 summer Assizes but kept at the Castle after agreeing to act as hangman.[94] Coates officiated at two executions in 1836 and 1837 but in November 1839 escaped from the Castle and was never recaptured.[95] Five months after the escape a hangman had to be

---

[91] The pamphlet trade could be highly profitable. Thomas Gent, a well known York printer, wrote in his autobiography that he had considerably expanded the few dying words spoken by Layer before his execution in 1723 and it had a run of sale for three successive days (quoted by Radzinowicz, op. cit, vol. 1, p 180-81).

[92] Surtees Society, Vol 40, *York Castle Depositions*, xxxv – xxxvi [In the seventeenth century] whenever there was a want of an executioner a condemned criminal was reprieved if he would accept the odious office;' It was probably difficult to get any except convicts to take the post, since hangmen were commonly held in general contempt and execration. When Curry the York hangman retired in 1835 the *Yorkshire Gazette* suggested that Jonathan Martin, the incendiarist who had fired the Minster in 1828 be appointed so that 'that notorious individual already execrated by all honest and good men may become the abhorrence also of all malefactors and dishonest persons.'

[93] This was in fact the second time Curry had been convicted of and sentenced to death for sheep stealing (having been previously convicted seven years before). Also known as Wilkinson his nickname was 'Mutton' Curry. (B. Bailey, *The Hangmen of England* (W.H. Allern, London, 1989), p 63).

[94] The first hanging at which Coates officiated was that of the Sheffield criminal Batty. His appointment appears to have been a last minute affair (c.f. *York Gazette*, April 2, 1836 ' some inconvenience arose in consequence of a person from Bradford who had been engaged as executioner in place of Curry, having declined to perform the duty. A substitute was, however found in one of the convicts who undertook the unpleasant task). In 1833 it had been reported by a local newspaper that a transport called Sowden was trying to get the office of Jack Ketch. He was presumably aware of Curry's impending retirement. Coates and William Doherty had both been convicted of dwelling house burglary at the Summer Assizes, 1835; both were sentenced to transportation; according to the Assize calendars Doherty had left the Castle by February 1836 but Coates was still there as late as July 1839.

[95] *York Gazette*, Nov 30, 1839 'on Thursday morning was discovered a very daring escape of prisoners from York Castle. [They] were James Coates ... William Marshall ... and William Sellers... On Wednesday evening the cells were all left apparently safe but early next morning it was found that the prisoners had in some manner at present not known escaped from them and scaled the outer walls by means of rope ladders

found to execute Bradsley convicted of parricide at the 1840 lent Assizes. Once again a convict was recruited. 'The executioner' reported the *York Gazette*, 'wore a prison dress. It is generally understood that he [is] a convicted felon now incarcerated in the Castle.'[96] He was later identified as Nathanial Howard, a coal porter. Howard acted as hangman until his death in 1853. By this time, due to age and infirmity, he was barely capable of performing the duties of the office and, had he not died, would probably have been dismissed. After him came a Maltby man, Thomas Askern who held office until 1874.

Like Calcraft, the Newgate hangman, Curry often fortified himself for his grim task with gin and was frequently jeered by the crowds at executions. In January 1813 he hanged 14 Luddite rioters for their part in the raid on Cartwrights' Mill (described by Charlotte Bronte in her novel *Shirley*).[97] In 1815 when he hanged Joseph Blackburn he placed the noose so carelessly that it dropped from its proper place; only after Blackburn's body had been convulsing for two minutes did Curry intervene and try and replace the rope in its original position which he eventually succeeded in doing.[98] On one occasion in 1821, when he had executions to perform both at the Castle and at the City Gaol (after the construction of a City Gaol in Skeldergate in 1807 city prisoners were executed behind it on the Baile Hill), he was jostled whilst he was walking from one venue to the other and drank so much that he was scarcely able to climb upon the scaffold and had even more difficulty getting the noose over the victim's head. At this the crowd began to shout and jeer 'Hang him. Hang Jack Ketch, he's drunk,'[99] to which his response was to shake the noose at the crowd and invite them to have a try.[100] On another occasion, at a multiple execution, he fell through the trap himself along with

---

made from bed rugs not far from Castlegate Lane end ... Coates is said to be a great adept at opening locks.' Of 59 prisoners who escaped from the Castle between 1824 and 1853 Coates was the only one to avoid capture. It is possible that a skeleton found when the perimeter wall of the prison was demolished in 1935 may have been his.'

[96] *York Gazette*, April 11, 1840.

[97] When passing sentence of death the trial judges had remarked that they 'might hang more comfortably on two beams.' Curry in fact hanged them in two batches, seven of them at 11 in the morning and the other seven at half past one: B. Bailey, op cit., p. 63.

[98] M Atholl, op. cit., p 76.

[99] Jack Ketch was the London hangman in the late seventeenth century. 'The nickname Jack Ketch was commonly used of every hangman who followed him for well over a hundred years, so great was the hatred with which he was remembered': B. Bailey, op. cit., p. 11.

[100] B. Bailey, op. cit, pp. 63-64.

his victims and emerged badly bruised to roars of laughter from the crowd. Askern was no more skilful than Curry: when he attempted to execute a prisoner called Johnson at Leeds in 1877 the rope broke and this was not the first bungled execution to which he had been party.[101]

---

[101] The incident, which was quite horrific, is described *The Times,* April 4, 1877, p 4c. 'As soon as the drop fell, the rope, which was an old one supplied by Askern, snapped, throwing the condemned convict Johnson to the ground where he lay groaning. After a delay of about ten minutes a newer and thicker rope was procured and fastened to the cross-beam. Johnson was then led from beneath the drop back on to the scaffold and turned off a second time. This time the rope held and after five minutes of convulsive struggling he expired.' The execution proved to be Askern's last. His other claim to notoriety is that he carried out the last public execution in Scotland when he hanged 19-year-old Robert Smith outside Dumfries prison on May 12, 1868.

CHAPTER TWO

Hanged at the York Tyburn 1750-1801

Between 1750 and 1801 thirteen people were hanged at the York Tyburn for Sheffield crimes and a Sheffield man was executed for a York burglary. They were:

Name	Age and occupation	Crime	Where committed	Date of trial; Judge	Date of execution	Disposal of body
1. Isaac Turner	Not known	Theft from linen drapers	Market Place, Sheffield	Spring, 1766, Bathurst J.	Saturday March 6, 1766	Not known
2. John Vickers	Not known	Robbery	Attercliffe (nr. the *Blue Ball*)	Spring, 1775, Gould J.	Saturday, March 30,1776	Not known
3. Frank Fearne	18, Apprentice File-smith	Murder	Kirk Edge nr. Bradfield	Spring, 1782, Eyre B.	Tuesday, July 23, 1782	Gibbeted Loxley Common
4. William Sharp & 5. William. Bamford	26, Labourer 28, Labourer	Burglary of dwelling	Sheffield	Summer, 1786	Saturday, August 19, 1786	Not known
6. John Stevens & 7. Thomas Lastley	Button-makers	Robbery	Lady's Bridge Sheffield	March, 1790 Buller J	Saturday, April 17, 1790	Not known
8. George Moore	Soldier	Burglary of shop at York	York	March, 1790 Buller J	Saturday, April 17, 1790	Not known
9. John Bennet	18, Apprentice	Riot and arson	Broom Hall, Sheffield	August 3, 1791 Thompson B.	Saturday, Sept 6, 1791	Not known
10. Spence Broughton	46, Highwayman	Mail Robbery	The Ickles,	March 24, 1792, Buller J	Saturday April 14, 1792	Gibbeted Attercliffe Common
11. John Hoyland	77	Bestiality	Attercliffe	Summer, 1793	Saturday, August 9, 1793	Not known
12. James Beaumont	Filesmith	Murder of cohabitee	A house in the Nursery	Summer, 1796, Lawrence J.	Monday, July 18, 1796	Given for dissection
13. Mary Thorpe	Servant	Murder of bastard child	Bridge Houses	March 14, 1800, Rook J	Monday, March 7,1800	Given for dissection
14. John McWilliams	28 Watchmaker	Forging bank notes	Sheffield	March, 1800 Rook J	Saturday, April 12, 1800	Not known

Isaac Turner, 1766 [102]

Isaac Turner was convicted at York Lent Assizes, 1766 of stealing goods from dwelling houses of Caleb Roberts and Matthew Lambert[103] in Sheffield Market Place. Left for execution by Mr Justice Bathurst, he was hanged at Tyburn on Saturday March 6, 1775 along with two other felons.[104]

John Vickers, 1775 [105]

At the York Summer Assizes, 1775 a grand jury found two indictments against John Vickers of Attercliffe. The first charged him and John Booth with robbing John Murfin of 3½d in money, a bad shilling, a breast of mutton and half a pound of butter, tied up in a handkerchief. The robbery was alleged to have been committed between 11 pm and midnight on Saturday, February 11, 1775 near the *Blue Ball*. The second charged that, on the same night, Vickers and three persons unknown robbed John Staniforth of 3s.6d in money, a sacking wallet containing horns for knife scales, a leg of mutton, 6 lb of sugar and some flax, the robbery being alleged to have taken place outside the *Glass House*.

It seems that Vickers was a member of a gang, preying upon customers emerging from public houses the worse for drink. It was his bad luck that the victim of the second robbery was a man to whom he had once been apprenticed and who immediately recognised him.

He was tried with Booth on the first indictment. He was convicted, Booth acquitted. Sentenced to death by Mr Justice Gould, he was hanged at Tyburn on Saturday March 30.[106]

---

[102] Knipe, op. cit., pp. 83-84. (Published in 1867 Knipe's work purports to be a *Register of the Criminals Capitally Convicted and Executed at the County Assizes* since March 1, 1379. Although useful it cannot always be trusted: at p 198, for example, the author states that there was a large assembly of spectators at the execution of Thomas Musgrave on April 6, 1839 when, in fact, there was no hanging and no crowd, Musgrave having been reprieved two days before.

[103] Roberts and Lambert were linen drapers.

[104] They were Thomas Taylor and Abel Hobson both convicted of burglary. Lydia Nicholson tried for receiving the goods which Turner had stolen was acquitted.

[105] Knipe, op. cit., pp. 88-89.

Although living in Attercliffe at the time of the robberies, Vickers had been born at Hemsworth Back Moor in Norton.

Frank Fearne, 1782 [107]

Frank Fearne was the son of a Bradfield farmer. Apprenticed in 1778 to a Sheffield file-smith[108] he soon showed himself to be an idle waster and many in the town predicted he would 'go to a bad gate.'

In early 1782 he called in the High Street shop of watchmaker, Nathan Andrews, claiming he could put some business his way: a watch club had recently started up in Bradfield and, if he visited the village, Fearne would introduce him to the members. Andrews said he would come once the club had twenty members. On Thursday March 18, Fearne had a half-holiday from work. With a knife and a pistol hidden in his pockets, he called on the watchmaker again. The club now had a score of members and, if he wished, he could take him to meet them that afternoon. Andrews agreed and shortly afterwards they set off.

At Kirk Edge a young man called Wood passed them on his way to work in the fields. He knew Fearne and bade him 'Good day.' It was by now around 4 pm. As soon as Wood was out of sight, Fearne dropped back, allowed Andrews to get a little ahead of him and then shot him in the back. As the watchmaker lay slumped on the ground, he went for him again, stabbing him with a knife and then smashing his skull with a hedge stake. After stealing the watches which Andrews had brought to show to the club members, he made off.

At dusk Wood finished work for the day and began to walk back to the village. As he did so he stumbled on Andrews' body. Shocked he went for help. A number of villagers went back with him and the body was carried to the workhouse. It was

---

106 He was hanged with William Bean and Matthew Normington who had been convicted of robbery at the same Assize.
107 Knipe, op. cit., pp. 91-93, C. Drury, *A Sheaf of Essays of a Sheffield Antiquary*, J W Northend, Sheffield 1929, p 118, *Sheffield Spectator*, Vol 9, No. 70, February 1971, pp. 58-59; *South Yorkshire Notes & Queries*, Vol. 1, p 173. File-smith and local poet, Joseph Mather (1737–1804), wrote a song about Fearne which is printed in Knipe, p. 93.

obvious that it was a case of murder but who was the dead man? His pockets were empty and there were no markings on his garments. Because of his sober dress - black coat, waistcoat and breeches, short black gaiters and white stockings - it was at first thought he was the local parson, but, as soon as Wood saw him in the light, he realised he was dressed identically to the man he had seen that afternoon with Fearne.

Back in Sheffield, Andrews' failure to return was already causing concern and, when news reached town that a man had been found murdered at Kirk Edge, the connection was made.

By now the finger of suspicion was pointing at Fearne. Not only had Andrews left Sheffield in his company, but he had been seen with him close to the place where the murder had been committed. The following night, a constable went to his lodgings in Hawley Croft, roused him from his bed and told him what was suspected. He protested his innocence but, when his room was searched, several of Andrews' watches were found. He was told to dress, handcuffed and taken to the Town Hall cells. A few days later he was committed to York to stand trial for murder.[109] During his short stay in the cells he was in surprisingly good heart, telling a friend who visited him there that he was confident that he would be acquitted because 'no-one saw it.' He was tried at the Summer Assizes, 1782 before Mr Justice Eyre. The jury brought back a verdict of guilty.[110] The judge, when passing sentence of death, directed that his body be handed over to the county hospital for dissection, but later had a change of mind and signed an order directing that it be gibbeted 'on a conspicuous spot on Loxley Common ... at a convenient distance from the highway.'[111]

---

[108] Drury, op. cit, p. 118. According to the records of the Cutlers' Company he was apprenticed to John Wilkinson of Folderings. But one account of the case speaks of him being apprenticed to Mr Ellis of West Bar Green.

[109] Whether he was committed for trial by the coroner or the West Riding magistrates is unclear; an inquest on the body was certainly held at the workhouse to which it was taken.

[110] Mr Wheat, a local solicitor, was paid by the Town Trustees £14.19.0 for conducting the prosecution (Leader, *The Records of the Burgery of Sheffield*, Elliot Stock, London, 1897, p 392 (entry for July 30, 1782).

[111] The full text of the order was 'I do hereby order that the execution of Frank Fearne be respited until Tuesday, 23rd day of July instant, and that his body instead of being anatomised shall be hanged in chains upon a gibbet to be erected on some conspicuous spot on Loxley Common in the parish of Ecclesfield in the county of York at a convenient distance from the highway.'

Fearne was executed at Tyburn on July 23 1782 along with three coiners.[112] It is said that he died gamely. Just before he was turned off he removed his shoes and tossed them into the crowd, shouting 'My master often said I'd die with my shoes on so I have pulled them off to make him a liar.'[113] He died hard after much struggling. Following the execution, a cart carrying his body set out for Loxley Edge where a gibbet post had already been erected.[114] It was gibbeted in front of a huge crowd most of whom had followed the cart from Sheffield.

On Christmas day 1797 the skeleton fell from the cage of the gibbet. The post, however, remained standing until 1807 when Mr Payne, on whose land it was, took it down. It is said that it was used to make a rough bridge across the river Loxley, but was later washed down to Sheffield in a flood and there salvaged by a builder who used it in the construction of a row of miners' cottages.

The murdered Nathan Andrews was buried next to his father in the Parish Churchyard.[115]

Sharp and Bamford, 1786 [116]

Of William Sharp and William Bamford nothing is known beyond their names and crime. They were hanged at the York Tyburn on August 19, 1786 for breaking into the house of Duncan McDonald, a Sheffield button maker, and stealing a quantity of horn combs and 7d in money. Sharp was 26 and came from Conisbrough. Bamford, a 28-year-old labourer, was from Clifton, Rotherham.

---

[112] They were John Cockroft (coining 1s); John Wood (coining 1s) and Thomas Greenwood (having in his possession tools for coining).

[113] Cf *Oxford English Dictionary*: 'To die with in one's boots or shoes or with one's boots on: to die a violent death spec. to be hanged' A similar story is told of John Carpenter, otherwise known as Hellfire Jack, executed at Newgate on April 4th 1805: to prove false predictions made in the past that he would 'die in his own clothes and shoes' he is said to have gone to the scaffold wearing old clothes and shoes, belonging to someone else, which had been brought in for him by a friend; see Charles Gordon, *The Old Bailey and Newgate*, 1905, p 349-50. According to Knipe, (op.cit., p. 191) when Ebenezer Wright was executed at the New Drop on March 30, 1833 he too kicked off his shoes on the scaffold.

[114] By Thomas Holdsworth, a local man, who was paid 15s by the Town Trustees for carrying it to Loxley Edge: see Leader, op. cit., p 394, entry for August 30, 1783. The rocks where the gibbet stood were for a long time after known as Gibbet Rocks.

[115] Drury, op. cit, p. 118: The father, Thomas Andrews had died on November 1, 1778 in his 61st year.

[116] Knipe. op. cit., 97-98.

Lastley and Stevens, 1790, Moore, 1790 [117]

On the night of Saturday August 29, 1789 the *White Hart* in Waingate[118] was packed with customers. Drinking in the basement were John Stevens, John Booth, Thomas Lastley, Michael Bingham and John Wharton. All five worked at Hoole's factory in nearby Lady's Walk, Wharton as a labourer the others as button makers. After a couple of hours or so of steady drinking, Wharton got up and announced that he was 'off home.' His wife kept a small shop in Chapel Street, Bridge Houses and he had promised her that he wouldn't be out long. The others protested and tried to stop him leaving but he dodged past them and escaped into the street. They decided to follow him and when he emerged from the market, where he had been making some purchases, they accosted him. 'Come back to the *White Hart*' they urged but he refused and walked straight past. On Lady's Bridge he went into a urinal leaving his basket on the pavement outside. When he came out the others had it; he tried to grab it back and there was then a short scuffle which ended with the button makers running off with his shopping.

They made for the *Barrel* in Pincher Croft Lane where Stevens lodged. It was after 11 when they got there but the house was still open. They ordered ale and finding some mutton in Wharton's basket asked the landlady to cook it. They were all expecting him to show up but he didn't. Having finished the mutton they put aside enough to pay him for the meat and parted, Stevens going to his bed in the attic of the Inn, Lastley to his wife in nearby Burgess Street and Booth and Bingham to their homes. At midnight the landlady, Mrs Marshall, locked up and retired to bed.

Wharton, in the meanwhile, had gone to Eyre, one of the town constables, and made a complaint. His concern at that stage was not to give the four into custody but merely to give them a fright and to get his shopping back. Eyre told him not to worry; he would soon settle the matter and give the lot of them a fright they would never forget to the end of their lives. The constable and Wharton parted in Fargate, Wharton walking

---

[117] Knipe, op. cit., 106-108, *Sheffield Advertiser*, April 1 and 9, 1790, *Sheffield Advertiser*, April 23, 1790, *York Chronicle*, April 2, 1790.

[118] According to Gell's *Directory of Sheffield, 1825* the *White Hart* was at 5, Waingate.

back to Bridge Houses and Eyre heading for Pincher Croft Lane. On reaching the *Barrel*, Eyre listened at the door and, having satisfied himself that the button makers were there, he walked off down the Moor as far as Little Sheffield to consider how best to proceed. He returned to the public house just after midnight. It was by now shuttered and in darkness. He hammered on the door and demanded admittance. Stevens, awoken by the commotion, came downstairs to find out what was happening. On seeing the constable, he pointed to a cupboard where Wharton's basket had been put. Eyre seized it and left without a word. He then set off for the home of Justice Wilkinson at Broom Hall, roused him from his bed and got him to issue warrants for the arrest of the four button makers.

Stevens in the meantime had gone across to Burgess Street to tell Lastley of the constable's visit. By now both were very frightened. After they had talked, Lastley decided to go for a walk to try and clear his head and think. At about 4 o'clock Eyre called at the *Barrel* for a second time, arrested Stevens and took him to the Town Hall cells. He went next to Lastley's house and being told that he was not there began a search. Just after 5 o'clock he discovered him hiding among the gravestones in the parish churchyard. He too was taken to the cells where, later that morning, Booth and Bingham joined him.

On the Monday all four were taken before Vicar Wilkinson and another magistrate for preliminary examination. Evidence was taken from Wharton, Eyre, Mrs Marshall and William Taylor.[119] Taylor had been in the *White Hart* on the Saturday evening and, like the prisoners, had ended up at the *Barrel*. He told the same story as they: that the whole matter had been intended as a joke and Wharton was not a penny worse off. All four were remanded until the following Friday when further evidence was taken. At the conclusion of the hearing Stevens and Lastley were committed to York Castle charged with robbing Wharton on Lady's Bridge of a basket containing a shoulder of mutton, a pound of tobacco, half a stone of soap, seven pounds of butter and 4d in money. Booth and Bingham were remanded for further examination and on October 28 they too were sent for trial.

---

[119] According to Knipe, op. cit., p. 104-05, Taylor was 'a tailor by trade who worked for Mr Sanderson in Change Alley [and] resided in Pinfold Street.'

The four were tried at the end of March 1790 before Mr Justice Buller. The landlord of the *White Hart*, the landlady of the *Barrel*, Taylor, Eyre and a number of others gave evidence. Counsel for the prisoners endeavoured to make light of the affair. The judge, however, summed up against them and, after an hour's deliberation, the jury brought back verdicts of guilty against Stevens, Lastley and Bingham who were immediately sentenced to death. Booth who, according to the witnesses, had been no more than an onlooker and had protested against the basket being taken, was acquitted. He was discharged and at once set off walking back to Sheffield where he arrived two days later.

When news of the result of the trial reached the town it caused a great sensation. No one had been expecting the accused to be convicted. Soon there was talk of Eyre (who was still not back from York) and Wharton having got up the prosecution with an eye to blood money.[120] After dark, a large angry mob gathered on Lady's Bridge shouting threats against Wharton. Hearing its approach, he and his wife ran off across the back fields beyond the Nursery.[121] Finding them gone, the mob broke open the door of the shop, smashed all its windows and set it alight. Soon it was gutted. The couple were never seen in Sheffield again; rumour had it that they had fled to Manchester.

Even at this stage few in the town thought that the sentence of death on the three men would be carried out. On the morning after the attack on Wharton's shop, the Master Cutler called a public meeting. A petition to the King was prepared which was signed by a large number of people including everyone of influence in the town. At 8 am the following day three of the town's leading citizens set off for London with the petition. They took the flying coach and reached the capital in four days. After consultations at the Home Office they secured the desired reprieve which was

---

[120] Cf the following verse from a poem quote by Knipe, op. cit., p. 108, which sounds like the handiwork of Mather, the Sheffield file-smith poet:

> 'We took John Wharton's basket and meat
> But not with an intent to keep;
> Like Judas he did us betray;
> For money he swore our lives away'

The statutory reward for securing a conviction for robbery was £40 and so Eyre and Wharton stood to gain £160 if all four accused were convicted.

[121] I.e. the Duke of Norfolk's Nursery which lay to the east of Nursery Street and from which that street takes its name.

immediately despatched by King's messenger. Due to flooding on the Great North Road in the Lincoln area the messenger did not reach York until April 19. He was too late. Stevens and Lastley had been hanged two days before. Bingham, however, was saved. Even before the reprieve was granted the judge had decided to recommend that he be pardoned on condition that he undergo transportation for life. On April 30 he was granted a free pardon.

Hanged with Lastley and Stevens was George Moore.[122] Moore came from Sheffield Park. He was a blade-forger by trade and also a notable prize-fighter, who had fought in front of large crowds on Crookes Moor.[123] In 1790 he enlisted in the 19th Foot who were at the time recruiting in Sheffield. Shortly after arriving at the regimental headquarters in York, he and three others broke into the shop of William Davis in the city and stole items of hardware.[124] Tried and convicted at the city assizes he was left for execution. From the condemned cell he wrote to his father asking him to visit. The father, old George Moore, who worked for Mr Saynor of Scargill Croft, had not the money to finance such a trip. However, his friends and neighbours got up a subscription and he set out. When he reached Brightside he stopped for a drink and soon he had drunk all his money away. Having done so, he turned back for Sheffield. He told his friends that he had thought the matter over and had reached the conclusion that he could have done no good for his son had he seen him.

The day before their execution Stevens, Lastley and Moore were present in the prison chapel when the Rev. Richardson preached the condemned sermon, taking as his text *Amos*, iv, 12 'Prepare to meet thy God.' All three are said to have manifested

---

[122] See Knipe, op. cit, p. 107, Leader, *Sheffield in the Eighteenth Century*, pp 52-53; *York Chronicle*, March 26, 1790.

[123] One of the highlights of his career had been a particularly desperate fight between him and a man called Dewsnap.

[124] Cf the following verse concerning Moore from the poem referred to in n. 16 above:

> I, George Moore, must tell you plain,
> I lose my life for little gain;
> For shopbreaking that shameful deed,
> It makes my tender heart to bleed;
> A harlot's company I did keep,
> To think of her that makes me weep;
> Through her I took to evil ways,
> Which is the short'ning of my days

contrition and 'a becoming resignation to their fate,' although this did not prevent Lastley declaring to the crowd at Tyburn that 'Wharton knew that there was no intention to steal.'

John Bennet, 1791 [125]

On Bastille day 1791 there was anarchy in Birmingham. A mob, angered by disloyal handbills circulating in the town, set out on the rampage, their target being all and any who were or were believed to be anti-King and Church. They fired the dissenters' Old Meeting House first and then set out for Sparkhill where lived Dr Priestley, the pastor of the meeting-house and a known sympathiser with the Revolution. Over the following days many other large houses in the area were attacked and fired, including Mosley Hall, the home of William Hutton. The riot was eventually put down with the assistance of a company of the 15th light dragoons despatched from Nottingham. The damage caused came to over £50,000.

Close on the heels of this riot came another at Sheffield. Although blamed at first upon 'persons recently arrived from Birmingham,' it was in fact the product of purely local grievances. In June that year, a number of land-owners, who included the Duke of Norfolk and the Rev. Wilkinson, the vicar and senior magistrate of the town, had obtained an Act for the enclosure of Crookes Moor and other waste and common land in Hallam, amounting to 6,000 acres in all. The Act was bitterly resented, not least because it was seen as depriving working men of their right to use the moor for shooting and recreation. *The Times* later claimed that so enraged were the lower classes by the enclosures that their cry was 'Liberty or Death.'

On July 13, commissioners appointed to carry the Act into effect arrived at the *Rising Sun* to survey the common. They were met by 'aproned cutlery workers' who drove them off with threats and violence. Over the next few days there were further

---

[125] Knipe, op. cit., pp. 169-70, *The Times*, July, 30, August 1 and 4, 1791; *Sheffield Register*, July 22, August 5 and 12, 1791, *York Chronicle*, August 26 and September 9, 1791; *York Herald*, 27 August, 1791, R.E. Leader, *Sheffield in the Eighteenth Century*, 2nd edn., Sir W Leng & Co, Sheffield, 1903, pp. 60-61, Carolus Paulus, *The Manor and Parish of Ecclesall*, J W Northend, Sheffield 1927, pp 29-33 and p 71; S. Johnson, *From Bailey to Bailey*, Sheffield 1998, pp. 4-5.

disturbances. On July 23 Joseph Ward, the Master Cutler, vicar Wilkinson and Vincent Eyre, the Duke of Norfolk's land agent, worried by the deteriorating situation, despatched a memorial to the Home Office requesting military assistance. In it they related how on several occasions mobs had assembled and driven off the enclosure commissioners and had threatened to fire the house of any landowner friendly to the Act and to lay open all enclosures already made in the district.

The Home Office immediately made arrangements for a troop of light dragoons to be sent from Nottingham. They arrived at noon on Monday, July 27. People swarmed into the streets to watch them ride by. The atmosphere was highly charged and many hung around the town centre to see what would happen. By 9 pm there were hundreds of people milling about in front of the *Tontine Inn*.[126] The trouble, which all had been expecting, erupted when Joseph Schofield, bailiff of the Sheffield debtors' gaol, arrested a man for debt outside the *Tontine*; the crowd at once intervened and freed him and he ran off.

Had Schofield had any sense he would have let the matter drop, but he didn't. He followed after the debtor and retook him near the gaol. The mob, seeing this, intervened and again set him free. Schofield now took refuge in the jail, which the mob had started to pelt with missiles (a pile of stones intended for pavement repairs provided a plentiful supply). Soon after, the crowd, who were shouting 'Pull it down!' forced the outer gates and began to beat on the door of the gaoler's house demanding the keys. These were passed out, the inner gate opened and the gaol's 19 or 20 prisoners released. At this point the dragoons arrived and the mob took to their heels. In the attack all the windows and shutters of the building had been smashed and a lamp at the entrance and part of the cypher DN[127] above the door broken.

---

[126] The *Tontine Inn* erected in 1785 stood in Dixon Lane. The construction costs were raised by a tontine, each subscribed nominating a life during the continuance of which (not exceeding the 99 years for which the ground had been leased) he was to receive an equal share of the rents and profits. In 1850 the Duke of Norfolk purchased the Inn, demolished it and built on its site the Norfolk Market: *Hunter's Hallamshire*, Virtue & Co, London, p. 199n.

[127] DN: Duke of Norfolk; the Debtors' Gaol was in Pudding Lane (now King Street).

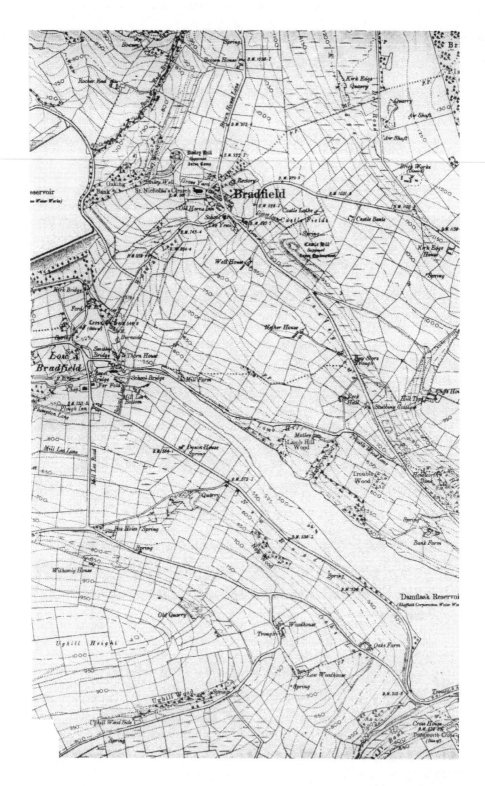

Map of Bradfield showing Kirk Edge where Frank Fearne murdered Nathan Roberts.

A print of the gibbeting of Fearne's body at Loxley Common. The gibbet site, which cannot now be identified clearly, lay well above the main road.

The Rev. Wilkinson, vicar and chief magistrate of Sheffield and the owner of Broom Hall.

The Tontine Inn which was used by the authorities as a command centre during the 1791 riots.

Broomhall Street today. The rioters swarmed along here as they headed for Broom Hall.

Broom Hall today.

Bridge Houses today. It was near this spot that Mary Thorpe murdered her child.

Once away from the gaol the fleeing rioters re-grouped and now set off for Broom Hall,[128] the home of Vicar Wilkinson. A harsh magistrate, a promoter of the enclosure Act (from which he stood to profit to the extent of 12 acres) and widely blamed for a recent widening of Church Lane, which had caused graves to be disturbed, he was deeply unpopular in the town. That evening he had been dining out on the other side of Sheffield and, as he was riding home, he was met some two miles from his house by his servant, John Gregory, who told him of the disturbances in town and said that he had come to escort him back. As the pair got near to the Hall they were met by another servant who told them that the mob were coming and urged the Vicar to look to his own safety. Seconds later they heard the mob coming along Backland Lane[129] (now Broomhall Street) shouting 'All in a mind.' Wilkinson and the two servants ran to the Hall. Inside the vicar found a letter waiting for him; it had been sent from the *Tontine* and warned of danger. After reading it, he got back on his horse and rode away, leaving Gregory in charge of the building.

Gregory put out the fires in the grates, closed the shutters and prepared for the worst. The mob now appeared on the green at the front of the house. They were shouting 'All in a mind' and one of them was playing a tambourine; they started to stone the house. Gregory at once retreated to the haystacks, a hundred or so yards away. Already hiding there was Henry Jenkins, the vicar's coachman. Some of the rioters were by now inside the house starting a fire in one of the downstairs rooms. After about ten minutes, Gregory and Jenkins saw three men approaching the stack garth.[130] They went to one of the stacks; two pulled off straw and the third set it alight using either a candle or a torch. As the stack caught fire, they shouted 'Damn it, there he goes.' They then moved to the second stack and fired that. They could be heard shouting 'Stick true.' Once four stacks were alight they retreated a short distance but soon returned shouting 'Stick true. All in a mind' and set fire to the rest. At this point the dragoons came clattering along the lane and the mob at once dispersed, many of them running into nearby woods.

---

[128] Broom Hall stands on the corner of Broomhall Street and Park Lane.
[129] Later the street name was corrupted to Black Lambs Lane. The rioters' route was presumably along Trippet Lane and thence by a lane to Broom Hall (see Fairbank's Map of Sheffield, 1771).
[130] Yard or paddock.

About ten minutes after they had gone, Gregory, who had taken refuge in the house of the Vicar's neighbour, Mr Spooner, emerged from his hiding place. The stacks were by now well ablaze and beyond saving and he went straight into the Hall. In the breakfast room there was a badly burnt mahogany table upon which books, pamphlets and newspapers had been piled and set alight The furbace around the room had been on fire and at one point along its length completely destroyed. One of those who had helped to extinguish the fire was Charles Clement. He had seen the mob go past his home in Church Lane and had decided to follow them. When he arrived at the Hall the dragoons, whom he had earlier seen pursuing rioters along Change Alley, were already there. He made his way inside the building, which was full of suffocating smoke and eventually managed, by copious use of water, to put out the flames.

On their way back into town the rioters re-grouped for a second time and now made for the house of Vincent Eyre. Some stones were thrown but the dragoons arrived and drove them off before any serious damage could be done.

The following morning the magistrates swore in hundreds of additional constables and two troops of heavy dragoons arrived from York. In the meanwhile there had been arrests. Those taken included John Bennet, an 18-year-old parish apprentice[131], William Ellis, Benjamin Johnson, Thomas Furniss and Ellis Froggatt. Bennet had been stopped as he was returning from Broom Hall. When in custody he had named Ellis as one of those involved. Johnson had been found in the early hours of the morning lying on the church-yard steps. Asked what he was doing he had replied that he dare not go home for fear of being taken. When an attempt was made to seize him he ran off but he was taken soon afterwards. Furniss had been arrested on suspicion of being involved in the attack on the town gaol.

That morning all five were taken before Colonel Athorpe,[132] the magistrate, at the

---

[131] Bennet lived in Waingate.

[132] Colonel R.A. Athorpe of Dinnington Hall, described by Mary Walton (*Sheffield its History and Achievements*, 5th ed. 1984, Amethyst Press, p. 137) as 'a peppery squire ... typical of his class and generation.' On August 4, 1795 during a riot in Norfolk Street Athorpe ordered troops to fire on the crowd which they did killing two persons on the spot. The riot was reported in the Sheffield *Iris*. The criticisms which he had made of Athorpe's conduct in that article led to the paper's editor being prosecuted for criminal libel. He was tried at the West Riding Quarter Sessions in January 1796 fined £30, sentenced to six months' imprisonment in York castle and ordered to provide sureties for his future good behaviour.

Tontine. After taking evidence, he committed them to York for trial, Bennet and Ellis on a charge of riot and arson, Johnson for riot and causing damage to the prison and the house of Vincent Eyre, and Furniss for riot and damage to the prison and assaulting Schofield. Another eight men were released for lack of evidence with a strong warning as to their future behaviour. None of those committed was over 19 years of age. They set off for York heavily laden with chains and with an escort of dragoons. They passed along the Wicker and through Attercliffe followed by friends, relatives and the usual multitude, and then over the common, onto Doncaster and thence along the Great North Road.

They took their trials at the York Summer Assizes on August 13, 1791 before Baron Thompson. At the start of the Assize the judge, in his charge to the grand jury, had spoken of the enormity of the offence with which the Sheffield prisoners were charged and of how utterly subversive it would be of all society if a mob were permitted wantonly and unprovokedly to assemble together and destroy the property of individuals and disturb the public peace. All such persons, he said, had no cause to justify or palliate their crimes since the laws were fully adequate to the redress of all real grievances and the most exemplary punishment awaited them and they would find, when perhaps it would be too late, that the little regard they paid to the laws of their country and the destruction of the lives and properties of individuals protected by those laws would bring the vengeance of the government upon them; [if] ... found guilty they would have no reason to expect mercy.

Indictments were duly brought in against Bennet, Johnson and Furniss. But against Froggatt the grand jury found no indictment and at the end of the Assize he was discharged by proclamation.

Bennet was the first to be tried. Crown counsel, in opening the case against him, told the jury that the prosecution had been undertaken by the government who were determined to spare no expense in bringing to justice those who should be guilty of the offence with which Bennet was charged; that they had selected him as a fit object for punishment, as being the person who had actually set fire to the house of the magistrate and, though on any other occasion, his youth might entitle him to some hopes of mercy, yet the enormity of his present offence was such that to save him would be to encourage crimes; he sincerely hoped that if the prisoner was found guilty his punishment would operate as a solemn lesson to the unthinking men who had been concerned in the riots in Sheffield.

The principal witness against Bennet was Ellis, who had been admitted King's evidence. Ellis claimed that, when he arrived at the vicar's house, he saw Bennet enter it, holding a lighting candle; inside he set fire to some books on a table and, after heaping coats onto the fire, climbed out of a window leaving the flames to take hold; he then went up the yard, still holding the candle but was back shortly afterwards, shouting 'We have set them on fire.' He was with two men, Davidson and Elliot, both of whom had absconded. In cross-examination he admitted he had been taken up as a result of Bennet informing on him. He denied entering the Hall himself. 'I watched through a window' he claimed. He said that Bennet had been in there for about five minutes. The only other Crown witness was William Slater who spoke of seeing Bennet and Ellis together after the mob had returned from Broom Hall; they were separated by a distance of about 400 or 500 yards when he saw them and the mob had gone.

Bennet offered no statement in his own defence but left the case to his counsel. His master John Walker was called. He had taken Bennet as a parish apprentice and he had three years left to serve. During the last months he had been very steady and he would take him back again if acquitted.

Slater's evidence, which afforded some slight confirmation of that of Ellis, appears to have been enough to satisfy the jury that the latter was telling the truth and they returned a verdict of guilty. Baron Thompson, passing sentence of death, told Bennet that the good government of the country required that he be shown no mercy.

The next prisoner put up was Benjamin Johnson. Three witnesses implicated him: Robert Cundall, John Hindley and John Brookfield. Cundall told the jury that he saw a man very like the prisoner throw a stone at the window of the gaol; he saw the men who were taken that night and noticed the prisoner amongst them and recognised him by his clothes. 'You are the man I saw throwing stones at the gaol last night,' he told him. 'Yes sir. I only threw one' was the answer. Hindley, who had a shop opposite the gaol, related how he had seen a man, whom he thought was the prisoner, stoop to th ground, pick something up and put himself in a posture as if throwing a stone; seeing the prisoner in court he was not positive he was the man but, when he saw him in his dirty clothes at the *Tontine,* he had been in no doubt. Brookfield, who had detained Johnson and taken him to the *Tontine,* said that Johnson had begged to be let go, saying that he had only been at Mr Eyre's and, if he would let him go home, he would never be concerned in any mob again. The only evidence offered on Johnson's behalf was that of William Newsome, a Greasborough collier, called as a character witness. He said he had known the prisoner since he was born and had 'never heard aught bad of him.' He was a quiet man who had a failing in his understanding and 'was ever considered weak in the head and easily persuaded.' He had had a blow behind his head when a boy and had never been right since. On hearing this, prosecuting counsel invited the judge to direct an acquittal which he did.

When Furniss, the last of the four prisoners, was brought up into the dock, prosecuting counsel announced that there was no sufficient evidence to convict him on the indictments which he faced and he was immediately acquitted.

Bennet was hanged on Saturday, September 6, along with John Minitor, a Rotherham man convicted of arson of a barn, and Abraham Robertshaw, a forger. On the Thursday before, Rev Overton had preached the condemned sermon in the prison chapel, taking as his text *Luke,* xviii, v 13 'God be merciful to me a sinner.'

One of the consequences of the riot was that Sheffield got its own garrison. In July 1792 work began on the construction of barracks on a site at Philadelphia beyond Shalesmoor, bounded by what are today Infirmary Road, Penistone Road and Barrack Lane. The new barracks were opened in 1794. Built of brick and stone they comprised a large parade ground and buildings and stables sufficient for two troops of cavalry (200 men). They had cost more than £2,000. White's *Directory* for 1833 explained to readers that they had been built

> 'as a means of keeping the peace and quelling any uprising and for the purpose of awing the threatening aspect of the people who had long been clamorous for reform in parliament and had several times evinced their joy on receiving intelligence of the successful progress of the French revolutionary armies.'

In 1849 they were replaced by Hillsborough barracks. The riots also left the town facing a bill of £561.15.1 ½ for costs and compensation.

Vicar Wilkinson lived on for another thirteen years.[133] An uninspiring cleric who had allowed the parish church to fall into dreadful disrepair, his reputation was not enhanced by an incident recorded by Leader:[134]

> A little girl in the street was incited to go up to a gentleman walking along and say,
>
> They burnt his books
> And scared his rooks
> And set his stacks on fire
>
> The child innocently went in front of the gentleman and bobbed a curtsy 'What my dear?' asked the Vicar for it was none other. The child repeated it. 'Yes, my dear,' said he, 'come along with me' and he, leading her by the hand, took her to the stocks to her great distress.

Spence Broughton, 1792 [135]

Spence Broughton was born in 1746 at Marton near Sleaford, the son of a prosperous farmer. By the age of 22 he had his own farm, paid for and stocked by his parents. Soon afterwards he married the only daughter of a local farmer, who brought with her a considerable marriage portion. At first the marriage was happy but then he took up with another woman. His wife, who by now had three children, sued for a separation. After this he gave himself to dissipation, spending his time in the company of gamblers and card-sharps and regularly attending horse races and cock fights. One of those he took up with was John Oxley who, as a boy, had worked in the stables and carried the letter bag on horseback from Wentworth House to Rotherham and back.

On January 24, 1791 Shaw, a London receiver of stolen goods, called at Oxley's house at 1, Frances Street, Tottenham Court Road. Having satisfied himself that Oxley

---

[133] James Wilkinson was the fourth son of Andrew Wilkinson of Boroughbridge and one of the daughters and co-heiresses of William Jessop of Broom Hall. He was appointed Vicar of the town in 1754. A tall and stately man, he was a fine amateur boxer and a mighty hunter. Unmarried he lived at Broomhall where he had a justice room for dealing with magisterial business. Mary Walton's verdict upon him (op. cit., p 137) was that 'as a shepherd of souls he was utterly inadequate.' He died on January 18, 1805 aged 74. There is a bust of him in the Cathedral.

[134] Leader, op. cit, p. 240.

[135] Knipe, op. cit., pp 111-128, *York Herald*, March 26, 1792, *The Times*, March 27. 1792.

was familiar with the road between Sheffield and Rotherham, Shaw told him that he wanted him and Broughton to rob the Rotherham mail. Oxley, who was strapped for money, readily agreed. At 10 the next morning there was a meeting at Shaw's house in Prospect Row. Present were Shaw and his wife, Close (who was, Shaw's partner in a London lottery office), Close's London mistress (he also had a home and a wife and children in Change Alley, Sheffield), Oxley and Broughton. The men went out and discussed the proposed robbery as they walked between Prospect Row and the *Dog and Duck*. Shaw gave Oxley and Broughton an advance of ten guineas and later that day they set off north. According to Oxley, they took the Nottingham Coach, which they boarded at *The Swan with Two Necks* in Lad Lane; Shaw, however, would later claim that they left on the Derby coach.

The following day they set off for Chesterfield on foot, hoping the coach would overtake them, but it was full and would not pick them up. They arrived in the town at between 8 and 9 pm on the 28th and stopped overnight at the *Three Cranes* where Broughton, who had stayed there twice in the past, was recognised by the landlady. They were late rising the next morning and it was after 11 when they left.

After dark on the evening of the 29th post boy, George Leasley, was driving the post cart from Sheffield to Rotherham when, at the Ickles about a mile and a half from Rotherham, a man, dressed in a smock frock and a cap, stepped out into the road and flagged him down. The man told him he must come with him and, taking the horse by the bridle, led it into a field. The lad was told to dismount, was blindfolded and his hands were tied behind him and secured to a hedge. He was told he must wait there and that in three or four hours someone would come to release him. After an hour or so he managed to free himself. His horse was tethered to the gate of the field but the mail-bag was gone. He only ever saw one man and, because of the dark, never got a good look at his face. However, there is little doubt that Oxley and Broughton were his robbers. Broughton later told an accomplice that Oxley had stopped the boy and he had opened the gate to the field.

After the robbery the pair set off for Sheffield on foot. Once they had put a little distance between them and the post boy, they stopped and searched the bag. They opened the letters but found only one thing worth taking, a bill of exchange enclosed in a letter addressed to Jonathan Walker of Masboro'. The bill, which was for £123.14.0 and in Walker's favour, had been drawn in Paris on January 14, 1791 by a French merchant, M. Virgelle, upon London merchants, Minet & Factor. Having pocketed it, they dumped the bag in a brook.

The robbers' route took them south to Chesterfield and then on to Mansfield. On the Saturday Broughton was seen in Chesterfield by a man he knew called Beresford but wouldn't stop, saying that he was in a hurry and had to get to Pontefract. By the time they reached Mansfield Broughton, who had gone lame in one leg, declared he could go no further. On the Sunday Oxley caught the mail coach at Mansfield Town End, travelled on it to Leicester and then to London. Broughton, however, stayed on in Mansfield.

Once back in London, Oxley set about turning the stolen bill into cash. He paid a man ten guineas to indorse it and then called on Shaw. The latter, having checked with the aid of a French dictionary that the bill was due, went with Oxley and Close to the Inner Temple Gateway. There Oxley approached a porter called Liske and sent him with the bill to the office of Minet & Factor in Austin Friars. Shaw followed at a distance, intending to warn Oxley should anyone come out of the office with Liske. But no one did. The porter was given a cheque drawn upon a bank in Lombard Street which he took and cashed. He received £123.14s which he handed to Oxley. He was given 18d for his trouble. Later that day, Oxley left £10 with Broughton's cohabitee, Mrs Hill, and then decamped with the balance to Leicester.

The Saturday following, Broughton arrived in London. Between the obelisk and Blackfriars Bridge he bumped into Close. He began at once to complain that Oxley had got the money from the bill and had gone off to Leicester cockings and said that he intended to follow him and get his share. Having caught up with Oxley at Leicester, he managed to get £40 off him and seems to have been satisfied with that.

On June 9 Oxley and Broughton were back in business robbing the Cambridge mail. The bag contained a number of bills including a ten guinea Stamford Bank Bill. On Monday October 16, 1791 a man offered the stolen bill at the shop at a silversmith's shop in Cheapside, in payment for a half guinea ring. When Metham, the shopkeeper, declined to take the note, the man, who was respectably dressed and accompanied by a lady, announced that he also wanted to buy a cream jug costing a guinea and a half. At this, Metham reluctantly agreed to take the note and gave him change The man and his companion then went into a number of other shops making small purchases which they paid for with bills stolen from the mail. When the bills were presented at the bank they were at once identified as having come from the mail and a search was mounted for the couple.

Two days later, Metham's eighteen-year-old shop boy was crossing Blackfriars Bridge when he was struck by the resemblance which a man, who had just ridden by on horseback, bore to the man who had passed the stolen ten guinea note. He immediately threw down his coat and the load he was carrying and chased after the man. Back over Blackfriars Bridge and up Fleet Street he ran and at Snow Hill managed to catch up with his quarry who was held up by heavy traffic. He followed him into a public house in Clerkenwell and there accused him to his face. The man, who was Oxley, ran off but was quickly caught and taken before Sir Sampson Wright at Bow Street. He told the magistrate that his name was Oxley and that he had had the bills of a Mr Shaw, who had asked him to get them converted into cash, which, being done, he gave the cash and the articles he had bought to Shaw at his house near Blackfriars Road. At the mention of the house, two Bow Street officers, Townsend and Jealous, at once set off there. Finding it empty they went in. Minutes later there was a rap on the door. They opened it and saw a stout, tall, athletic man standing there. He asked if Shaw was there but, on being invited in, took to his heels. After a long chase he was finally caught near the *Dog and Duck* in St George's Fields. He was searched and in his pocket was a handful of banknotes. [136] It was Broughton. The officers took him to Bow Street and announced to the magistrate 'We have got him.' 'What Shaw?' asked the justice. 'No, a fellow worth a hundred Shaws,' they replied.

Broughton and Oxley were remanded in custody and on Monday June 25 brought up for examination. Shaw, realising the game was up, had in the meanwhile agreed to go King's evidence. He told the magistrate that, about a fortnight before the robbery of the Cambridge mail, Broughton and Oxley had come to his house in Prospect Row

---

[136] The Bow Street runners kept the money they took from him for themselves.

saying that they were planning to rob the Cambridge mail near Bournebridge and had asked him to join them. He had refused but had told them that he was due to go to Cambridge on business anyway and would make some inquiry about the mail and tell them what he found out. He took the fly to Cambridge from the *Queen's Head* in Gray's Inn Lane and, by making enquiry at the post office and keeping watch for several nights, he had learned how the mail was carried. Once he was satisfied he knew how the system operated he returned to London and passed on the information to Broughton and Oxley. They again pressed him to join them; again he declined. On June 8 they left London. Two days later he received a message asking him to meet them at the *Cannon* coffee-house in Portland Road. There Broughton gave him a handkerchief with notes in it, which he said were from the robbery, and later that night he, Shaw, buried them in his back garden. A few weeks later he dug up the notes and took them to an empty house which he owned at 9, Middle Row, Holborn. There, in the presence of Broughton and Oxley, the handkerchief was untied. Each took a few bills for the purpose of negotiating them and over the next two or three days they passed £150 worth. There was about £400 in Bank of England notes, half of which were endorsed *P.post - Wood & Dowling* and, thinking it unsafe to try and negotiate them bearing that endorsement, Oxley removed the ink using spirit of salts, a trick which he had learned whilst working in a lottery insurance office. Questioned as to what was taken from the Cambridge mail, Shaw declined to answer precisely but admitted that there were twelve to fourteen Stamford Bank £10 notes, £400 in Bank of England notes, a bill for £750, another for £350 as well as other bills which had either been passed or burned. The total, on his admission, came to between £5000 and £10,000.

During the examination, Oxley appeared anxious to make full disclosure (presumably in the hope of being admitted evidence against Broughton and Shaw) and gave detailed information about the robbery of the Rotherham mail. He also alleged that on May 28, at Shaw's suggestion, he and Broughton had robbed the Aylesbury mail but said that all they had got were a few bank notes which were of no use. Shaw, who had put up £14 towards the costs of the venture, had complained that he was out of pocket on it and suggested they carry out the robbery of the Cambridge mail to reimburse him. Oxley claimed that Broughton had carried out the Cambridge robbery and had been wearing a smock frock as at Rotherham. Afterwards both of them took the mailbag to a small wood where they opened the letters; after removing the bills they buried the letters and then walked to Biggleswade, where they caught Nottingham and Leeds coach into London. The Cambridge mail boy, when called, gave it as his opinion that it was Broughton, not Oxley, who stopped and robbed him, thus corroborating Oxley.

On November 1, Broughton and Oxley were further examined. Leasley, the Rotherham post boy attended, but was unable to identify either. At the conclusion of the hearing both were committed for trial in custody, Broughton being remanded to Newgate and Oxley to the Clerkenwell Bridewell.

Oxley, however, managed to escape from Clerkenwell. Bricklayers, who had been repairing some outhouses in the prison yard, had left a ladder there. Oxley, who was a prisoner in the Lodge where the confinement was less strict than in other parts of the gaol and was only lightly ironed, used the ladder to climb out of the yard. As he was making his way over the leads of an adjoining house, he dislodged an earthen pan placed there for the birds. The noise alerted the occupants who immediately raised the alarm but, despite this, he got away. The escape was highly suspicious and looks pre-planned: the ladder left in the yard was just a little too convenient and how, without help, could he have got down from the leads or rid himself of his irons? After giving his pursuers the slip, Oxley was foolhardy enough to turn up at a gaming house in Norris Street, Haymarket and then at the *One Tun* public house. Only with difficulty was he persuaded by the landlord to make himself scarce. He was never seen again.

Following the escape, Broughton was removed by writ of *habeas corpus*[137] from Newgate to York to stand trial for the Rotherham robbery at the Spring Assizes, 1792. Oxley, being still at large, he was tried alone. The trial took place on Saturday, March 24 before Mr Justice Buller. It began at 9 am and did not finish until 10.30 pm. Shaw was admitted King's evidence and it was he and Close whose testimony damned Broughton. It was put to Close in cross-examination that he had told a man called Woodward that Broughton knew nothing of the robbery and that he had only accused

---

[137] A writ of *habeas corpus ad testificandum* directed to the gaoler was a means of securing the attendance in one county of a prisoner held in custody in another.

him for fear that Oxley would impeach him and take his life, but he denied it. Although it was clear that both Shaw and Close were out to save their necks at the expense of Broughton's, the prosecution were able to prove that Broughton was in Chesterfield on the day before and the day after the robbery and that he had been in Mansfield on the Sunday following. It was also proved that Oxley and Broughton had been seen together at the cockings in Leicester in early February. At the conclusion of the judge's summing up the jury immediately brought in a verdict of guilty. Mr Justice Buller then addressed Broughton. He told him that he had been convicted (on the clearest evidence that could possibly be produced) of a crime which must have been long premeditated and which in its consequences was most baneful to society, of a crime of such a nature as to leave him without a shadow of hope that he could receive mercy on this side of the grave. His punishment would not however end at the place of execution. In order to deter others from offending in a like manner his body would afterwards:

> be suspended betwixt heaven and earth (as unworthy of either) to be
> buffeted by the winds and storms.

Having recommended Broughton to make the best use of the little time allowed to him in this world he then passed sentence of death upon him. According to the press 'Broughton, throughout the whole awful scene, behaved with the utmost decency and fortitude.'

After his condemnation he spent a good deal of time trying to bring the other prisoners, who were under sentence of death, to a state of repentance. He told the clergyman, who attended him, that he did not rob the mail but was in Nottingham at the time. He claimed that, by giving information against his accomplices, he could have done them much harm, but that he preferred to die than to be guilty of such dishonourable conduct. He said he freely forgave those who had been instrumental in his death. His only support during his confinement was his mistress, Mrs Hill. On the eve of his execution, he wrote to his wife expressing remorse for his treatment of her and urging her to teach their children the ways of religion and warn them against gaming.[138] He was hanged on Saturday, April 14 1792 with four other men; John Lucas, Thomas Crawshaw, Thomas Stearman and Joseph Brierly (all convicted of burglary). When climbing into the execution cart he said 'This is the happiest day that I have experienced for some time.' On his way to Tyburn he prayed very earnestly. With his last breath he said he died a murdered man.

The gibbet on which Broughton's body was to be hung was made in the Sheffield Nursery and was fixed in position on Attercliffe Common on the day of the execution. It was erected some 200 yards from the *Arrow Inn.* On the Sunday a crowd, estimated at 40,000, gathered to await the arrival of the corpse and by 8 pm the common was like a fair. It arrived at around 2 o'clock on the Monday morning by which time most of the crowd had dispersed. The body in its wire cage was quickly hoisted to the top of the gibbet and in a few minutes was swinging in the wind.

The money which Drabble, the landlord of the *Arrow*, took from beer sales on the Sunday was, he would boast in later life, the making of him financially.

In May, 1792 a respectably dressed woman visited the Inn and sat for a considerable time in the window overlooking the gibbet, weeping. From the description given by landlord it appears that it was Broughton's widow.

As late as 1817 the whitened bones of the dead robber could still be seen with the remnants of his clothes fluttering in the breeze. In 1827 Mr Henry Sorby of Woodburn bought the land on which the gibbet stood and soon after had it dismantled and the post put in his coach house. Its removal was not before time. By the 1820s, so far from serving as a deterrent, the gibbet had become a target for horseplay by local youths. In 1825 one of a group of potters from the Don Pottery at Swinton, whilst passing the gibbet late at night, threw a stone at the skeleton, knocking off a couple of its fingers. He pocketed them and the next day used them in the manufacture of a bone china jug (in 1871 the vessel was sold in London for £4).[139] From around the same period comes

---

[138] The letter is in Appendix 4.
[139] 'It appears that a party of Don and Swinton potters who had been to Sheffield for a carousel and stayed there till the early hours of the morning were, when not sober, returning over the moors when, on passing the gibbet where the gaunt skeleton of the malefactor still hung, as it had for some years, in chains, one of them saying 'Lets ha' a rap at him' picked up a stone and threw it knocking off the bones of two of the fingers.

a tale of a youth carrying a bowl of broth up to Broughton at midnight for a bet.[140]

On the April 21, 1792 the Post Office put out a notice offering a reward for Oxley's recapture:

GENERAL POST OFFICE
April 14 1792

At the lent Assizes 1792 for the County of Cambridge an indictment was found by the Grand Jury against Spence Broughton and John Oxley for robbing the Cambridge Mail near Bournebridge on the 9th June last; and at the same Assizes for the County of York, an Indictment was likewise found against them for robbing the Mail between Sheffield and Rotherham on the 29th January 1791, on which last Indictment Broughton was tried and convicted.

Oxley escaped out of Clerkenwell Bridewell on the 31st October last. He is about 25 years of age, 5 feet 10 inches high, pale faced, rather pitted with small pox and his nose turned a little to the right.

Whoever shall secure the said John Oxley and lodge him in any of the Gaols of this Kingdom within three months from the date hereon will be entitled to a Reward of ONE HUNDRED POUNDS to be paid immediately on his commitment.

By Command of the Postmaster-General

ANTHONY TODD Sec.

Early in 1792 there were reports that Oxley had been seen in the neighbourhood of Rotherham. These rumours went unheeded until the following appeared in the *Newark Herald* for Wednesday January 30, 1793:

On Friday last was found dead, of hunger and cold, in a barn on Loxley moor above Sheffield a man who had been seen for a few weeks before wandering about in that neighbourhood in the evenings but had concealed himself in the day time. It appeared, upon examining him, that his legs were marked and cut about the ancles as if he had been manacled with heavy prison irons; from which circumstance and from his avoiding with the greatest care the sight of any person, it is conjectured that he had

---

These were picked up and carefully carried home as trophies of the exploit, and some time afterwards, when trials in the manufacture china were being made, they were brought out, calcined and mixed with some of the body of which the identical jug is made'

The Don Pottery was at Swinton, and very few specimens of its china are known, the output at the works being principally earthenware.

The china body of this particular jug was mixed by Godfrey Speight and Ward Booth and it was painted by Taylor Booth: see Charles Drury, *A Sheaf of Essays by a Sheffield Antiquary,* 1929, p 120 (extract from the *Art Journal*).

[140] *S Yorkshire Notes and Queries*, Vol 2, p 6 letter: "A Sheffield workman called Smithers laid a wager with a companion named Mathers that he (Mathers) dare not take a basin of broth at 12 pm to the skeleton of Spence Broughton. The wager was accepted and the broth carried up a ladder by Mathers at 12 o'clock one night. Smithers secreted himself behind the gibbet and when Mathers (after placing a ladder near the gibbet) took up the broth to Spence Broughton's skeleton he said 'I've brought thee some broth, Spence lad.' Smithers answered, 'It's too hot,' to which Mathers replied 'Then blow on it lad."

broken out of prison; and that, dreading the consequences of a discovery, had preferred perishing as above to mixing any more with mankind. Turnips partly eaten were found in his pockets and about the place where he lay. He was slenderly made, had very black hair and was rather low in stature; had on a blue coat and other apparel decently good; silver plated buckles and silver studs on his shirt wrists marked D E. A person residing at Darnall near Sheffield, who was well acquainted with Oxley, declared that the man found in the barn was none other than John Oxley, the confederate of Broughton, although he did not see the body, but from the description given in the papers on the coroner's inquisition so exactly corresponding with the dress he wore at Darnall where he had seen him (Oxley) some weeks before. Oxley told him he had been across the common to look at Broughton; and had at about that time applied to his friends in the neighbourhood of Rotherham for assistance to enable him to leave the country, but which appeal met with a prompt refusal. Close used occasionally to come to the *Arrow* and on one occasion the conversation turned upon the probability of the body found in the barn being that of Oxley 'As sure,' said Close, putting his hand on Drabble's shoulder, 'as Broughton's bones are swinging yonder (pointing to the gibbet) so sure are those of Oxley in a solitary corner of Bradfield Church yard.' He (Close) mentioned at the same time the name of a notorious gambler in London, a great companion of Oxley, whose initials corresponded with the studs found on the shirt wrist bands.

Broughton, with a street and a railway station named after him, remains arguably Sheffield's most famous criminal.

John Hoyland, 1793 [141]

In July, 1793 John Hoyland of Attercliffe was committed for trial at the Assizes charged with bestiality. Aged 77, he was a harmless old man who had brought up a large family. For some years he had been the butt of his sons' violence, they habitually taking his wife's part in quarrels and regularly thrashing him so severely that he 'frequently was weeks together with bruises upon him.' He was accused by two Sheffield labourers, John Hunt and William Warburton, who claimed that on July 15 they had seen him copulating with an ass. Few in the town doubted that the charge was false and brought for the sake of 'blood money.'[142] But a York jury believed his accusers and Hoyland was convicted and sentenced to death. He was hanged at Tyburn

---

[141] See Knipe, op. cit, p 129, *Sheffield Iris*, July 19 and August 2, 1793, *The Times*, August 21, 1793, 3d.

[142] A number of seventeenth- and eighteenth-century statutes offered those who prosecuted felons to conviction a reward, varying, according to the crime, from £10 to as much as £40. There was an obvious potential for abuse and it was not unknown for men to be entrapped into or falsely accused of crime for the sake of a £40 reward. This had happened in 1756 in the notorious *McDaniel* case (1756) 19 St. Tr. 745 and was still happening as late as the 1820s. Rewards gained by false accusations were called 'blood money'

on Saturday August 9. Before he was turned off he insisted, as he had done from the time of his arrest, that he was innocent and declared that he would not change places with the men who had sworn his life away.

James Beaumont, 1796 [143]

On the night of Monday May 9, 1796, at a house in the Nursery district of Sheffield, James Beaumont strangled Sarah Turton the woman with whom he was living.[144] He then made his way round to Barley-field where his estranged wife kept a shop intending to kill her too, but she, alarmed by his wild appearance, wisely refused to let him in. Shortly after, he was arrested and duly committed to York for trial. His case came on at the summer Assize, 1796 before Mr Justice Lawrence. He was convicted, sentenced to death and his body ordered for dissection. Visited by his wife in the condemned cell Beaumont told her that, if he had listened to her, he would not have ended up as he had. He was hanged on Monday July 18. According to Knipe, his widow lived many years afterwards in a very creditable manner. A filesmith by trade, Beaumont left several children.

Mary Thorpe, 1800 [145]

In September 1799 a heavily pregnant young Ecclesfield girl travelled into Sheffield where she took lodgings with a widow named Hartley. She told her landlady that she was married and that her name was Ashford. Over the weeks which followed, the lodger, who was in fact single and whose real name was Mary Thorpe, kept herself very much to herself. On the third week in November she gave birth to a male child, a

---

(see e.g. *The Times*, February 24, 1818 'Blood Money'). In 1818 fixed statutory rewards were replaced by rewards at the court's discretion.

[143] See Knipe, op. cit., pp. 132-33, *York Herald*, July 16 and 23, 1796 and *Hull Advertiser*, July 23, 1796.

[144] This area lying close to the Wicker was where the Duke of Norfolk had his Nursery and it was from this that present day Nursery Street takes its name. Knipe says that the house where the murder was committed was the second house from the white rails coming into Sheffield.

[145] See Knipe, op. cit., p. 137, *Sheffield Iris*, December 17, 1799, *Sheffield Local Register*, March 7, 1800, *The Times*, March 20 and 21, 1800, *Hull Advertiser*, March 22, 1800 3c; *Hull Packet*, March 18, 1800 3b; *York Herald*, March 15 and 22, 1800, T.R. Lemon, *York Castle in the Nineteenth Century*, p 196. Cases

female friend assisting in the delivery. A week later she left her lodgings, telling Mrs Hartley that she was taking the child to her sister's at Derby, where it was to be nursed, and that she was catching the evening coach. Once clear of the house, however, she headed not for the inn, from which the coach left, but for Ecclesfield.

The following morning the body of a child was found in the river at Bridge Houses.[146] It had clearly been murdered. Tied around its neck was a tape; the tape had been wrapped three times around the neck and knotted each time; attached to the end of it was a heavy stone. The child was male, wrapped in a cloth and had a distinctive birthmark. When the widow Hartley was shown the tape and the cloth she had no doubt: the child was that of her recently departed lodger.[147] A surgeon called to examine the body confirmed that it had been strangled.

Mary Thorpe was quickly tracked down by the parish constable and arrested at her father's house on the pretence that she had left a child chargeable to the parish. She denied having had a child. On November 27 an inquest was held.[148] The jury at the close of the evidence brought in a verdict of murder against the young woman and the coroner, John Foster, committed her for trial at the next Assizes.

Her trial took place on March 14, 1800. According to the report in the *York Herald*,[149] when called on for her defence, she acknowledged that the murdered child was hers but said that she had delivered it to a man to take to nurse. A York antiquarian, however, maintains that she admitted her guilt 'but said that she was ill and delirious and knew not what she did;' he adds that 'it was proved that she suffered from milk fever but not sufficiently to destroy her sanity.'[150] It is clear from the newspaper reports that she was 'respectable looking' girl whose plight excited a good deal of sympathy amongst the spectators in court, but her defence, whatever it was, cut

---

such as that of Mary Thorpe were far from uncommon at this era; details of a Welsh case from 1805 which has more than a passing similarity to Mary's case are given in Appendix 6.

[146] The *Sheffield Local Register*, March 7, 1800 gives Bridge Houses as the place where the body was found. *The York Herald* March 22, 1800 says the body was found near a bridge about a mile from Sheffield.

[147] According to the *Hull Packet*, March 18, 1800, 3b the reason her act did not remain long undiscovered was that 'several female friends were convinced of her pregnancy and knew of the delivery.'

[148] This is the committal date given in the Assize Calendar; but contrast the *Sheffield Iris* for December 27 which describes her as having been committed 'last week.'

[149] *York Herald*, March 22, 1800.

[150] Thomas Rede Lemon, *York Castle in the Nineteenth Century*, T Saunders, York, 1931, p 196.

no ice with the jury who convicted her. [151] When Mr Justice Rook passed sentence of death upon her 'she bore it with great firmness and curtseyed very lowly to the court before she left it.'[152]

After sentence she displayed great contrition and acknowledged the justice of her punishment.

She was hanged at Tyburn on Monday March 17th and her body delivered to the county hospital for dissection. She did not die alone. Executed at the same time was Michael Simpson who had been convicted at the same Assize of murder by poisoning. Simpson continued to assert his innocence up to the moment when he was turned off, 'which fact,' according to Knipe, 'was proved eighteen months afterwards by the confession of the wretch who did the deed.'[153]

The identity of the father of Mary's child was never established, although it is said that 'he was far above her in circumstances and ... had taken advantage of that elevation to tempt her on to her destruction.'[154]

John McWilliams, 1800 [155]

Convicted at the same Assize as Mary Thorpe but hanged three weeks later was 28-year-old John McWilliams.

McWilliams came from Doncaster and was a watchmaker and engraver by trade.[156] On the evening of January 11, 1800 he arrived in Sheffield on the Doncaster coach. He immediately went into a local public house where he bought a drink and asked for a bed for the night. Told they had no rooms, he drank up and left. Shortly afterwards, one of the serving girls, while clearing up, found a bundle of bank notes lying under the

---

[151] *Hull Advertiser*, March 22, 8c 'a decent respectable looking young woman'; *Hull Packet*, March 18, 1800, 8c 'a very neat and respectable looking young woman'; cf Lemon, op. cit, p 196 'in person she was extremely prepossessing.'
[152] Thomas Rede Lemon, *York Castle in the Nineteenth Century*, p 196.
[153] Knipe, op. cit., pp. 137-38.
[154] Lemon, op. cit., p. 196. Her case bears more than a passing similarity to that of Mary Morgan (as to which see Appendix 6).
[155] Knipe, op. cit, p. 138, *Sheffield Iris*, January 17, 1800, *The Times*, March 21, 1800 3c, *York Herald*, March 22, 1800, *Hull Advertiser*, March 22 and 29, 1800, *Hull Packet*, March 25, 1800.
[156] According to the *Hull Advertiser*, March 22, 1800 3c, McWilliams had at one time been employed by a Hull shoemaker called Stanley.

chair in which he had been sitting. She took it to the landlord. Knowing that forged bank notes had been turning up in the area, he immediately sought out Dyre, the town constable. A search was set afoot and at ten o'clock McWilliams was tracked down to another public house where he had taken lodgings. The constable was taken up to his room and forced the door. As it swung open, McWilliams was seen trying to hide a bundle of bank notes. The notes, which had all been forged from the same plate, were drawn on the Sheffield and Rotherham bank. There were a hundred of them, some filled in, some not. When McWilliams was searched he had on him two watches, one of which he had bought a few days before and paid for with three forged bank notes.[157] He had been caught red-handed.

He was taken before the town magistrates and on January 17 committed for trial charged with forging and uttering 'divers promissory notes for one guinea each purporting to be Sheffield and Rotherham Bank promissory notes.'[158]

By the time he took his trial, the Crown had traced one of McWilliams' accomplices, a Doncaster butcher named Townrow. He told the court that he had received from McWilliams a hundred one guinea notes to pass off, forged from the same plate as those the subject of the charge. He had been promised seven shillings for every note he paid away. He managed to put off some of the notes but then an alarm went up and he immediately destroyed the rest. He claimed that McWilliams had offered to show him the plate from which the notes had been printed and that, when the alarm had gone up, he had asked him to get two good guinea notes of other country banks. This evidence made what was already an overwhelming case stronger still and the jury convicted without leaving the jury box.[159]

Sentencing McWilliams to death, Mr Justice Rook left him in no doubt that he would be left for execution.[160] He was hanged at Tyburn on Saturday April 12th 1800 together with 35-year-old William Dalrymple and 25-year-old Sarah Bayley, convicted respectively of bank robbery and uttering forged bank notes.[161]

---

[157] *York Herald*, March 22, 1800.
[158] *Assize Calendar*.
[159] *York Herald*, March 22, 1800
[160] *The Times*, March 21, 1800.
[161] Knipe., op. cit., p. 138

It is certain that McWilliams was an old offender. Indeed, according to the *Hull Packet*, had he not been convicted, the proprietors of a Huddersfield bank were ready to go before the grand jury to seek an indictment against him for forgery of their bank notes.[162]

---

[162] *Hull Packet*, March 25, 1800, 3b; the bank was that of Messrs Perfect, Seaton Brook & Co.

CHAPTER THREE

Hanged at the New Drop, York, 1802-1864

In 1801 the county magistrates resolved that Tyburn should no longer to be used for executions: criminals would henceforth be hanged on a portable drop at the back of the Castle.

Name	Age and occupation	Crime	Where committed	Date of trial; Judge	Date of execution	Disposal of body
1. Samuel Paramar	70, occupation not known	Rape of a girl under 10	Sheffield	Summer, 1807 *	Saturday, August 8, 1807	Not known
2. Mark Bramah	21, occupation not known	Rape of a girl under 10	Sheffield	Summer, 1815 **	Saturday, August 5, 1815	Not known
3. William King	30, edge tool maker	Murder of cohabitee	Arundel Place, Sheffield	July 29, 1817 Wood B	Thursday, July 31, 1817	Given for dissection
4. James Mosley	31, table knife cutler	Murder	Outside *The Harrow* public house, Broad Street, Park	March 18, 1822 Holroyd J	Saturday, April 6, 1822	Not known
5. Isaac Charlesworth	22, occupation not known	Robbery	Hyde Park Quarry	July 21, 1825 Hullock B.	Saturday, August 13, 1825	Not known
6. Martin Slack	18, apprentice brace and bit maker	Murder of his bastard child	North Street, West Bar, Sheffield	Spring 1825, Hullock B	Monday, March 30, 1829	Given for dissection
7. Charles Turner 8. James Twibell	both aged 19, occupations not known	Robbery	Nr. Manor Lane, Sheffield	March 24, 1831 Parke J	Saturday, April 30, 1831	Buried in the Parish Church-yard, Sheffield
9. Thomas Rodgers	32, labourer	Buggery	Sheffield	March 29, 1834 Alderson B	Saturday, April 26, 1834	Buried in St Mary's Church-yard, Castle-gate, York
10. William Allott	35, dairy farm manager	Murder of cohabitee	Upper Heeley	April 4, 1835 Alderson B	Monday, April 6, 1835	Given for dissection
12. Charles Batty	28, ex-soldier	Cutting and wounding with intent	Cush Yard, Mill Sands, Sheffield	March 7, 1836 Parke B	Saturday, April 2, 1836	Buried in St Mary's church-yard, Castle-gate, York
13. Thomas Williams	29, basket-maker	Murder of fellow workman	Silver Head Street, Sheffield	July 15, 1837 Coltman J	Saturday, August 12, 1837	Buried within precincts of York prison
14. Robert Nall	33, machine fitter	Murder of wife	Beehive Lane off Glossop Road, Sheffield	March 18, 1842 Coltman J	Saturday, April 9, 1842	Buried within precincts of York prison
15. Alfred Waddington	21, grinder	Murder of his bastard child	Cutlers' wood nr Heeley	December, 20, 1852, Talfourd J	Saturday, January 8, 1853	Buried within precincts of York prison
16. James Barbour	21, travelling salesman	Murder	Midhill, Black Bank, Sheffield	December 21, 1852, Talfourd J	Saturday, January 15, 1853	Buried within precincts of York prison

* The judges this Assize were Chambre J and Wood B.   ** The judges this Assize were Bayley J and Richards B.
It is not known which took the criminal list.

Paramar, 1807 [163] and Bramah, 1815 [164]

The first Sheffielder to die on the New Drop behind the Castle was 70-year-old Samuel Paramar, convicted at the Summer Assize, 1807 of raping a girl under ten and of assaulting another child with intent to rape.[165] Both offences were committed on June 21, 1807 and the children must have made prompt complaint for the accused was committed for trial only five days later.[166] He took his trial before Baron Wood who had no hesitation in leaving him for execution. He was hanged on Saturday August 8, 1807 along with John Robinson who had been convicted of murder at the same Assize.[167]

Eight years later, 21-year-old rapist Mark Bramah suffered the same fate.[168] His victim was a young girl called Eleanor Marson Darwin. Convicted at the summer Assizes he was executed on Saturday August 5, 1815 together with George White, another child rapist.[169]

William King, 1817 [170]

At around 6 o'clock on the morning of June 4, 1817 a neighbour saw 30-year-old edge tool maker William King pacing the pavement outside his workplace in Furnival Street, looking agitated. 'How are you?' he called across. 'I am but poorly, John,' replied King.

Half an hour later the neighbourhood was woken by a woman screaming. The screams were followed by the sound of blows and then by loud groaning. The cries

---

[163] Knipe, op. cit., 144; *Hull Packet*, July 21 and 28, 1807, *York Herald*, July 11, 1807.

[164] Knipe, op. cit. 155; *Hull Packet*, July 18, 1815.

[165] The girls were called Hannah Cowley and Maria Hobson (*Assize Calendar*). The newspapers regarded the details as too indecent to report: see e.g. *Sheffield Iris*, July 21, 1807 'The circumstances of this case, however they might amuse licentious curiosity, are so infamous and horrible that we declined publishing the account which we have received.

[166] *Assize Calendar* (the committing magistrate was H. Parker).

[167] Knipe, op. cit, p. 144.

[168] He was committed for trial by Hugh Parker JP on May 9, 1815 (*Assize Calendar*).

[169] White was 50 years of age and came from Snainton. Knipe, op cit., p.135.

[170] Knipe, op. cit., 156; *Sheffield Iris*, June 10, 1817, *The Times*, June 16, August 1 and 12, 1817 and *York Herald,* August 2, 1817.

which had come from King's house in Arundel Place brought neighbours running into the street to see what was amiss. The street door of the house was locked and there was blood running down the glass of the first floor bedroom window. The door was broken open and George Woodcock, who lived two houses away, rushed up the stairs to the bedroom. There he found King standing by the bed with a bloody poker in his hand; on the bed lay the body of Sarah Trippet, with a little child near her bloodied head. 'Good God!' he shouted. 'What is the matter? What have you done?' King's answer was to go for him with the poker. Woodcock fled and, on reaching the street, told the crowd outside to guard the door while he went for the constable. Hearing a child cry out another neighbour, John Goodlad, now made to go inside. 'Good God, he is murdering his children. Will nobody follow me up the stairs to prevent him?' he asked. But no one would.

Minutes later King, in response to shouts for him to come down, emerged from the house and backed against a wall where he stood holding the poker raised. Goodlad, who had by now returned armed, quickly knocked the weapon from his hand and together with another neighbour detained him. Shortly after this the constable arrived.

'What have you been doing?' he asked King.

'I've murdered my wife and children.'

'For what cause?'

'Jealousy. I did it with a poker and, if the deed were to do again, I would do it.'

'Have you been drinking?'

'I was in the *Swan with Two Necks* [171] last night and came home at ten o'clock.'

While King was being questioned two neighbours, John Young and Mrs Halley, went back into the house. In the bedroom they found a three-month old baby lying next to its mother and a 4-year-old boy sitting upright by her head; one child had a head wound. The injured woman, dressed only in her shift, looked as if her hair 'had been dipped in a blood kit.' Young thought he could detect signs of life and ran down to get help for her and Mrs Halley followed with the children. On hearing that she was still alive, King said 'I hope not.' He was then handcuffed and taken off to the Town Hall cells.

Sarah Trippet died before the surgeon arrived. When he examined her body, he saw that her face was badly disfigured. There were five large contusions to the head and an open fracture at the back of the skull, out of which brain matter was protruding. It was obvious that she had been violently beaten with a weapon.

The following day the county coroner held an inquest. After the evidence of the neighbours and the surgeon had been taken, King was asked what he had to say in his own defence. 'Damn your eyes!' he replied, behaving as though deranged. The inquest jury took little time in bringing in a verdict of murder and the coroner signed the warrant for his commitment to York.

His case came on at the summer Assizes, 1817 before Baron Wood. Prosecuting counsel, Mr Maude, in opening the facts to the jury told them a little about the history of the relationship between the accused and his victim. They had met five years before when Sarah was lodging with a respectable family in Sheffield. Notwithstanding that she was already married to a soldier serving in Wellington's army, she set up home with King and bore him two children. (According to *The Times* report, before consenting to live with him, she had written to the regiment in which her husband was serving and had received a reply telling her that he had been killed. Satisfied with this information she had moved in with the prisoner). Shortly before the murder King discovered that the husband was still alive (the soldier named in the casualty lists was another man of the same name). Maude told the jury that it was the husband's return to Sheffield, which had led to King learning the truth. He claimed that the two men had struck a bargain under which Sarah was to remain with King.

The same witnesses, who had given evidence at the inquest, were then called. King, who had no counsel, had nothing to ask them but the judge took pains to inquire of the neighbours whether he had ever displayed signs of madness prior to the killing. On this point they were unanimous: he was a man given to drinking and, when in drink, often flew into rages but that was all. Halley, his next-door neighbour, told the court:

> He knew nothing particular about King's understanding, except that he was rather sullen and fondish of ale. He followed his trade regularly and was considered sensible. He had never heard that he and his wife

---

[171] The *Swan with Two Necks* was at 28, Furnival Street.

quarrelled though he sometimes used to swear at her. He had been prevented from working for some time by a hurt in his hand.'

'Did the prisoner ever appear out of his mind?' asked the judge. 'He never did,' replied Halley.

At the close of the Crown evidence, King who, throughout the trial, had 'appeared gloomy and in a state of despondency approaching despair,' was asked for his defence. He answered in a low voice 'I have nothing to say.'

The judge having summed up, the jury returned a verdict of guilty without leaving their box. Baron Wood turned to address King:

> 'After a long and patient investigation you have been found guilty by a jury of your country of the crime of murder. The crime is ... the most horrid that can be committed by a criminal or punished by the law; but in your case it was accompanied by circumstances of peculiar atrocity. The woman whom you have most cruelly destroyed was a person with whom you cohabited and to whom you ought to have afforded protection. Instead of this, you not only murdered her but seemed to exult in the deed and to carry your malice even beyond death. The act which made everyone shudder produced no impression on you but a desire to renew it. Pray, therefore to God, during the short period you have to live that he may extend mercy to you in another world which you refused to one whom you ought to have protected in this.'

He then passed sentence of death and directed that King's body be given for dissection. King was taken from court betraying no signs of either contrition or emotion. In the condemned cell he appeared to be 'in a kind of melancholy stupor' and the clergy could make no impression upon him. He was hanged on Monday July 7, 1817 dying penitent, if Knipe's account is to be believed.

James Mosley, 1822 [172]

At about 4 or 5 o'clock on the afternoon of August 3, 1821 a group of grinders, who had been out of town looking at timber, stopped off for a drink at *The Harrow* public house, Broad Street, Sheffield Park. They had a room to themselves and stayed there drinking for several hours. In another room, were James Mosley and his friends. After the grinders had been in the house for some time, one of them went to the landlady and purchased a Banbury cake.[173] Another of the group, called Beuley, then decided that he fancied a cake and went to the bar and picked up one which Mosley had either just paid for or was in the act of buying. Mosley flew into a rage and went to hit Beuley but was restrained. He left and went to his brother in law's butcher's shop where he stole a knife. Shouting 'Damn him I'll stick him,' he set off for the public house. There he took up position near to the entrance with the knife hidden under his smock frock. About half an hour later the grinders emerged and, as they walked past, Mosley lunged at Beuley with the knife. The blow missed him but struck and wounded his companion, John MacKay, who immediately collapsed. MacKay was taken to the Sheffield Infirmary where he lingered on until September 3 when he died.

Mosley was arrested and, on March 16, 1822, stood trial at York for murder. As prosecuting counsel[174] began to open the case, it at once became plain that the Crown might have difficulty proving that the stab had caused Mackay's death. He told the jury that he believed the evidence would show that Mackay was, at the time of the stabbing, suffering from a fatal disease, but it was the Crown's contention that the blow had accelerated his death and, if it had, even by half an hour the prisoner was guilty of murder. When Thomas Waterhouse, a surgeon from the Infirmary, gave evidence, it was obvious that the Crown case was indeed in trouble. The dead man was, he said, suffering from heart disease, which could have caused his death at any time even without his having been stabbed, and there was nothing which caused him to think that his death had been caused or accelerated by the wound. After this evidence, Mr Justice Holroyd had no alternative but to direct the jury to acquit Mosley. The prisoner's triumph was, however, short lived. The Crown immediately went before the grand jury and obtained an indictment against him under Lord Ellenborough's Act for cutting and stabbing Mackay with intent to murder.

The following Monday, Mosley was brought back into court and arraigned on the new indictment. Again he pleaded not guilty. The trial lasted some five hours. Three witnesses were called on his behalf in an attempt to prove that he had been 'ill-used'

---

[172] Knipe, op. cit., p 165-66, *York Herald*, March 9, 16, 30 and April 13, 1822, *Sheffield Independent*, March 23, 1822.

[173] A kind of cake, filled with mincemeat, supposed to be made at Banbury.

[174] Mr Maude prosecuted; Mr Williams and Mr Jones appeared for the prisoner.

and provoked by the grinders, but their evidence was contradictory. The jury were clearly not impressed for, after a mere five minutes' deliberation, they brought in a verdict of guilty. Mosley was sentenced, together with the other capitally convicted prisoners, on the afternoon of March 23. The judge told him that his case was

> 'attended with such aggravating circumstances, in going to fetch a knife which he secreted and in laying in wait to wreak his vengeance on a man with whom he had had a trifling quarrel, as clearly showed his malicious intent. The safety of the King's subjects required that no mercy should be extended to him.'

He was hanged on Saturday April 6, 1822, together with William Roberts who had been convicted of highway robbery. On the scaffold both men joined in the chaplain's prayers with great fervour. Mosley, who left a wife and two children, showed great firmness but Roberts, once the cap had been drawn over his face and the rope placed around his neck, trembled so much that he had to be supported until he was turned off.

Isaac Charlesworth, 1825 [175]

On July 5, 1825 Joseph Cropper travelled over to Sheffield from Halifax to help remove the furniture of a Methodist Minister. He finished work at around 10 pm and then called in at the *Coach and Horses* public house in Water Lane, where he asked for a pint of beer. He was refused, the landlady telling him it was too late to fill for strangers. However, a group of four men who were drinking together and had seen what had happened, invited him to join them and persuaded the landlady to serve him. He was soon in conversation with his new companions. He told them he was from Halifax and asked if they could tell him where Grace Hanson, a woman whom he had known there, lived. They said they could and two of them offered to show him her house. He accepted the offer and left the public house with them.

He was taken through a number of side streets until at last they arrived at a quarry in Sheffield Park near Dyer's Bridge.

---

[175] Knipe, op. cit., p. 174, *The Times*, July 26, 1825, *Sheffield Independent*, July 30, 1825.

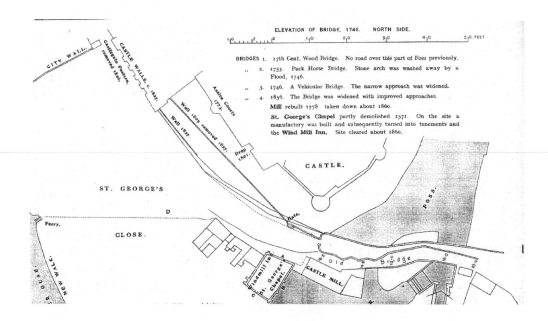

The site of the drop behind the castle is clearly shown.

The only known photograph of the site of the drop.
The gallows was erected in the alcove. The condemned emerged on to it through the
black doorway on the left hand side of the alcove.

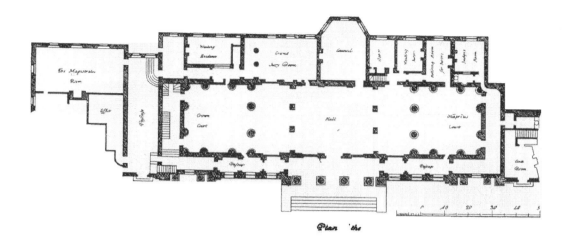

Court-house plan - The doorway through which the condemned emerged onto the scaffold can be clearly seen at the left hand side of the plan.

The Castle today - A court-house extension now stands on the side of the drop.

An ACCOUNT of the TRIAL, EXECUTION, &c. of

Isaac Charlesworth,

(Aged 22)

Who suffered Death, on the NEW-DROP, behind the Castle of York,

On SATURDAY, August 13th, 1825,

For Robbing JOSHUA CROPPER, on the Highway, at Sheffield.

IN a country like England, whose population is so great, and where the temptations to deviate from the paths of rectitude are so numerous, it is highly necessary, now and then, for the good of society, to make examples; but it seldom happens, except where the case is attended with aggravated circumstances, and it has rarely fallen to our lot to record one of deeper die than the present; but if any thing could deter men from the perpetration of crime, the awful fate of this young man ought to be a sufficient example to make them relinquish their evil ways, and tread in the paths of honesty.

Mr. MAUDE stated the case on the part of the prosecution, and called Joshua Cropper, who stated that he lives at Halifax. On the 5th of July he went with a horse and cart to Sheffield, to remove a minister and his family from Halifax to that place. He got there about seven o'clock in the evening, and having taken some refreshment, he went into the town to purchase some articles of hardware, after which he walked about the town, having never been at Sheffield before. About ten o'clock he went into a public-house in Water-lane, and asked for a pint of ale; the landlady said it was too late to fill for strangers. The prisoner and three other men were sitting in a room drinking, and they asked the witness to partake with them, and afterwards called for a pint of beer, which the prosecutor paid for. Witness entered into conversation with them, and inquired if they knew one of the name of Grace Hannah, a person who had come from Halifax to reside there; they said they knew her very well, and offered to go with the witness to her house; he accepted the offer, and two of the men took each of them an arm. They went through a number of streets, and at length came to a quarry, but far from Dyer's Bridge, into which they took him, and he had no sooner entered it than one of the men quitted his arm, and at the same moment he received a violent blow on the head with some instrument; the blows were repeated several times until he became insensible; he struggled as much as he could, and cried out Murder; his pockets were rifled and turned inside out, and there was taken from him a £t. note and 14s. in silver. He was covered with blood; and when he came to himself, he found that he was supported by a stranger. It happened, fortunately for the purposes of public justice, that a person of the name of Green happened to be near the place, and heard the cries of the prosecutor, and almost at the same moment a man ran out of the quarry, and passed him, having a hat in his hand, and one also on his head. He was followed almost instantly by another man, who was knocked down by Green; the man who was knocked down called on his companion for assistance, who returned, and after looking steadfastly in the face of Green, (who said to Charlesworth) " I know thee, thou shalt hear of this another day," pulled an instrument out of his pocket, and struck him on the side of the head, and then ran off. The blow brought him to the ground. He, however, soon recovered his feet, and ran about fifty yards further. The man who was running away threw the hat from him, but Green was so much exhausted with the blow and loss of blood, that he fell again on the ground. At this critical moment, a chaise-driver, of the name of Tudsbury, who had also heard the cries of Cropper, came to the spot and lifted up Green; he also picked up the two hats. Tudsbury called for the watchman, who proceeded with him to the quarry, followed by Green, where they found Cropper lying apparently dead; blood was issuing in great quantities from his nose, mouth, and ears. When he came to himself, he identified the hat. Green stated the person who was running away with it, and whom he had seen coming out of the quarry, was the prisoner; and a marble pestle was found about an hour after by the watchman, near the place where Green had been knocked down, an instrument which was proved to have been in the possession of the prisoner at six o'clock that evening. There were a number of other corroborating circumstances attending to establish the guilt of the prisoner. The Jury, without hesitation, found a verdict of GUILTY.

The day after his trial, Mr. BARON HULLOCK, in a most impressive manner, pronounced sentence of death upon him, when his Lordship informed him, that his case was attended with such acts of cruelty and aggravation, that he could not possibly quit the city without leaving him for execution. As the prisoner left the bar he said, " Please ye, my Lord, the last words I shall say on the scaffold will be, they (the witnesses against him) are perjured men, both of them."

Since his trial he behaved himself in a very becoming manner, was very fervent in his devotions, praying earnestly to Him, who alone has power to forgive sins, through the atoning blood of his Son, our Lord and Saviour Jesus Christ.

On Friday a most excellent sermon was preached by the Rev. Mr. Flower, the Ordinary, from the following text:—15 Chap. St. Luke, 10th Ver. " Likewise I say unto you, There is joy in the presence of the angels of God over one sinner that repenteth."

At the appointed time, he was led from the place of confinement to the Drop, attended by the Sheriff's Officers, and after praying a short time with the Ordinary, was launched into awful eternity, amidst a number of spectators.

On Saturday, August 19, 1786, a person of the name of Charlesworth, was executed at Tyburn, near this City, for highway robbery, committed under circumstances similar to the above.

J. Kendrew, Printer, Colliergate, York.

Broadsheet on sale in York following Charlesworth's execution.

What remains of Hyde Park Quarry today. This was almost certainly where Charlesworth committed the robbery for which he was hanged.

The Bee Hive public house where the inquest into the death of Mary Nell was held.

The Waggon & Horses public house, Upper Heeley in the early nineteenth century.
It was here that the inquest into Martha Hardwick's death was held.

The Waggon & Horses today.
The present building dates from the second half of the nineteenth century.

It was in this quarry where his two companions set upon him. [176] He was knocked to the floor, beaten about the head and left lying bloody and unconscious on the ground. When he came to he found that his money[177] and hat had been taken. Before being knocked down he had had shouted 'Murder.' His shouts had been heard by John Green who, shortly after, had seen two men running from the quarry, one carrying a hat. He struck the second man as he ran past knocking him down. At this, the first turned back, pulled a pistol out of his pocket and hit Green on the side of head with it.[178] The force of the blow knocked him to the ground and, although he managed to pick himself up and give chase, after about fifty yards he collapsed, exhausted and bleeding. A chaise driver, named Sudsberry,[179] who had also heard Cropper's shouts, now arrived on the scene. He helped Green up and took possession of two hats and a pistol which were lying nearby. They then made their way to the quarry where they found Cropper lying, bleeding with his pockets turned out. They assisted him to his feet and went for the constable.

Two witnesses said that the pistol which the first robber had dropped belonged to a local man, Isaac Charlesworth.[180] He was arrested the following morning, had had nine shillings in silver on him and said he had slept the night in a stable. He was shown to Green, who identified him as the man who had run from the quarry carrying a hat.[181] *The Times* report of the case suggests that there were other witnesses 'who identified [him] as being near to the spot at the time.'

---

[176] The quarry was in all probability Hyde Park Quarry. Dyer's Hill Bridge no longer exists; it was destroyed in the great upheaval caused by the building of the Sheffield Midland railway station in 1876. Dyer's Hill was a steep street leading up to Granville Street from the river Sheaf and the bridge, which took its name from the street, led over the river to the foot of Pond Hill. When the bridge was in existence the river ran much closer to the foot of Park Hill (S.R. Davey, *Crossin' O'er*, Parker Press, Sheffield, 1984, p 76).

[177] He had on him a Halifax bank note and 14 shillings in silver.

[178] Lemon, op. cit., p 685 claims that the blow was struck with a marble pestle.

[179] Some reports give his name as Tutbury

[180] Edgeley, one of Charlesworth's workmates, said he had seen it in his possession the previous month. Another witness called Southey claimed that he had seen the prisoner with it on the afternoon of the day of the robbery.

[181] Green may have known Charlesworth prior to the attack; one press report has him telling Charlesworth he knew him prior to the latter striking him with the pistol and Charlesworth knew enough about him to put to him that he had been convicted of felony, which he admitted.

Charlesworth was tried and convicted before Baron Hullock at the York Summer Assizes, 1825.[182] Sentencing him to death the judge told him that his case was attended with such acts of cruelty and aggravation that he could not possibly quit the city without leaving him for execution. He implored him to seek, by prayer and repentance, that mercy from his Creator which it was in vain for him to expect to receive from men. As he was taken from the bar, Charlesworth said 'Please ye, my lord, the last words I shall say on the scaffold will be that I have been murdered by means of perjured men.'

After his conviction, attempts were made to persuade him to name his accomplice, but he would not and the man was never caught.[183] He was hanged on Saturday August 13, 1825. He was just 22 years old.

Martin Slack, 1829 [184]

In 1826 fifteen-year-old Martin Slack took up with a girl called Elizabeth Haigh. He was an apprentice brace and bit maker and lived with his parents, five sisters and brother in Norfolk Lane; she lived with her parents in North Street, West Bar.

In summer 1828 Elizabeth became pregnant. The parish overseers, anxious to prevent the child becoming a burden on the poor rate, made her take affiliation proceedings against Slack. She having named him on oath as the father, a warrant was issued for his arrest. Unable, when brought before a magistrate, to offer sureties for his appearance at the West Riding Quarter Sessions to answer her suit, he was committed to the Wakefield House of Correction. His family could have prevented this by putting up bail for him but, being bitterly opposed to the liaison, refused to do so. After five weeks, however, his father relented and gave the required security.

On his release from prison, Slack called on Elizabeth and asked her to marry him. She agreed and the banns were actually read but his parents then stepped in. Being

---

[182] He was committed for trial on July 10, 1825 by H. Parker JP.
[183] Lemon, op. cit., p, 685 is highly critical of the failure of the Sheffield police to track down the second man. 'Where,' he asks 'was the landlord or landlady of the house they drank at? Could not he or she state who was the companion of Charlesworth on that night? Could not the officers trace who were Charlesworth's usual associates?'
[184] Knipe, op. cit., 179-83, *Sheffield Independent*, November 29, 1828 (inquest) and April 4, 1829; *Sheffield Iris*, March 28, 1829; *The Times*, March 30, 1829.

under age, the lad required their consent to marry and they made it clear that they had no intention of giving consent and continued to try to persuade him to give up the girl.

On October 19, 1828 Elizabeth gave birth to a baby girl. Shortly afterwards her affiliation suit came on for hearing and Slack was ordered to pay a weekly sum for the child's maintenance. This he bitterly resented. He continued to visit, however, and, according to Elizabeth, appeared much attached to the child, bringing toys for her on one occasion. An incident, which her brother-in-law Joseph Wells had witnessed on the Friday before the child died, had, however, left him in no doubt that Slack in fact disliked the infant: offered the baby to nurse he had angrily refused to take her, saying he wanted no such thing near him, a piece of churlishness which led Wells to tell him that he was 'an unnatural father.'

On the evening of Saturday, November 1, Slack called round at Elizabeth's house and stopped with her until about ten o'clock. As he was leaving, he asked her what time she would be up the next morning. 'Early,' she told him.

She got up on the Sunday shortly before 7 am and took the child downstairs to suckle it in front of the fire. As she was doing so, Slack arrived. She placed the baby on a squab[185] and went up to dress. She was on the stairs when she heard it scream. Rushing back down, she found Slack sitting in a chair holding the child in his arms. She took it from him and was about to put it to her breast when she saw smoke and something, which looked like brimstone, coming out of its mouth. She tried to comfort it and, in doing so, got some of the fiery liquid on her own cheek and arm. It burnt. She asked Slack if he had given the child anything. 'No, it's just sick. Give it some water.' She screamed back 'You've poisoned her.' 'If you are going to scream, I shall leave,' said Slack and, without another word, did. By now her brother, who had been asleep in the room in a chair, was awake. Her screams had also brought her father downstairs. As he reached the bottom stair, Slack was just going out of the door.

Elizabeth's married sister, Mary Wells, who lived across the road, had also heard the screaming and hurried over. She found Elizabeth cradling the baby in her arms and crying hysterically. 'He has poisoned my child,' she kept repeating. Mary took the

---

[185]   A settee.

baby off her, noticing as she did so, that the strings of its cap were burnt and there was liquid running out of its mouth. Some of it fell on her gown and took the dye out of it.

Mr Jackson,[186] the surgeon, was sent for and at 7.30 his assistant, Charles Lewis, arrived. He realised at once that the child was extremely ill: it was foaming at the mouth and there was a smell of *aqua fortis*.[187] He gave it warm water to dilute the acid and then magnesia and carbonate of potash. At first, the child seemed a little relieved but soon became worse. Lewis decided to seek the help of local surgeon, James Hardy.[188] When he arrived at 8.30 the baby was moribund. He administered further medication, but to no avail, and soon after it died. He, too, thought that the appearances pointed to the child having been given acid. Present when it died were Slack's parents.

Slack was apprehended that afternoon at Upper Heeley by John Waterfall, the parish constable. Waterfall noticed that there were burns on his fingers and marks on the left breast of his coat, on his waistcoat and on the inside of his waistcoat pocket. Slack told him that they had been caused by cutting wood. He was at once taken into custody and his clothing seized.

On the Monday, Hardy conducted a post-mortem examination of the body. The mouth had been completely destroyed, the windpipe was badly burnt and the stomach was highly inflamed. He thought that death had been caused by a corrosive poison[189] and that the marks on Slack's clothes were acid burns.

Later that day an inquest was held before Mr Andrew Hardy, one of the county coroners. He took evidence from Elizabeth and her brother. Slack was then brought in and their depositions were read to him. He declined to put any question to either but merely stated that he had not given the child anything. The next witness called was his workmate John Condon. He told the court that, shortly before the child's death, Slack had told him that he wondered that druggists sold *aqua fortis* as it would poison

---

[186] Probably Mr William Jackson of 18, Bank Street.
[187] Nitric acid.
[188] Of 84, Fargate.
[189] In 1819 a Devon woman, Frances Clark, killed her newborn child by giving it acid. Tried at three successive assizes she was each time acquitted on a technicality (see D.R. Bentley, *Select Cases from the Twelve Judges' Notebooks*, J. Rees, London, 1997, pp 125-32). It seems unlikely that Slack had heard of the case.

anyone.[190] There had been some joking in the workplace about Slack having to go to Wakefield again because of the child, but Slack had denied he would have to go. At this point Slack interrupted: 'That was because my master would pay the money for me.' Evidence was then taken from Elizabeth's father, sister and brother in law, from the constable and from the medical witnesses.

Once the depositions had been signed the coroner told Slack that, if he had any communication to make to the jury, now was the time for him to make it and cautioned him. He replied that he was sorry that the accident had happened but false evidence had been given against him by several of the witnesses. He went on to say that he called at Haighs' on the Sunday morning; Elizabeth had given the child to him while she went upstairs, it had begun to cry and she had come down and screamed at which he said he would go away. Later that day he went to see a fellow apprentice who was sick. He then learned that Waterfall, the constable was looking for him, went to find him and was arrested by him. The burn marks on his clothes had been there a long time. The coroner summed up the case and the jury, without retiring, returned a verdict of murder against Slack. The coroner immediately signed the committal warrant and exhorted Slack to lose no time in preparing for the worst. After the investigation which had just taken place, there could, he feared, be no reasonable doubt that he had been the author of the death of his own child. According to press reports, during the inquest Slack appeared unmoved 'his conduct throughout exhibiting the greatest firmness and self possession.'

The case caused a great sensation in the town. On December 13, the *Sheffield Independent* published a letter from a local clergyman blaming the murder upon loose morals and the failure of masters and of working class parents to ensure that those in their charge received a Christian upbringing.

Slack took his trial at the York Spring Assizes, 1829 before Baron Hullock. The same witnesses were called as before the coroner. Mr Cottingham, who had been retained as counsel for the prisoner, sought in cross-examination of Elizabeth and her

---

[190] At the Assizes Condon is reported to have added that on the day before the child's death Slack had told an absurd story about an Irish woman being poisoned by taking *aqua fortis* to warm herself when travelling (*Sheffield Independent*, April 4, 1829).

family to establish that they held a grudge against him for failing to marry her. Having elicited that no bottle was found at the Haighs' house after the prisoner had left, and that Slack did not use *aqua fortis* at his place of work, he suggested to Mr Hardy, the surgeon, that the appearance of the stomach might have been caused by inflammation rather than poison. Hardy would have none of it. 'Not in so short a time,' he replied. Slack, who was dressed in mourning and had remained completely unmoved when Elizabeth burst into loud sobs at the conclusion of her evidence, was then called on by the judge for his defence. 'Well my lord,' he answered, 'I am not guilty of the crime for which I am now arraigned at the bar and the evidences which have come against me have sworn falsely, as false as can be sworn here.' The judge then summed up and the jury, after a few minutes' deliberation, brought back a verdict of guilty.

Asked why sentence of death should not be passed upon him, Slack replied 'I am not guilty. I am a murdered man, a quite murdered man.' Baron Hullock then turned to him and exhorted him to seek God's forgiveness.' 'I have no reason to go upon my knees for mercy,' Slack shouted back, 'I am innocent. The mother of the child gave it something in a cup and then said 'Leave the house, the child is poisoned.' I went away and went to see a fellow apprentice who was ill at Hemsworth. I met Waterfall the constable as I returned. He said I was his prisoner. I replied very well I would go with him. I declare my Lord that what they swore against me at Sheffield was false and that they have sworn falsely against me here today. The Lord is with me and he will save my soul because I am innocent.'

'I can hold out no hope of mercy to you,' Hullock told him. 'That does not trouble my mind,' said Slack, 'I know the girl is guilty.'

The judge then proceeded to pass sentence of death and ordered that after execution Slack's body be handed over for dissection. Immediately he had done so, Slack shouted back 'Well, my lord, that is just what they wanted. They said at Sheffield I should be hanged and dissected but they have got it by false swearing. I say you are an unjust judge. You have not done your duty in sentencing me, an innocent man, to die. I am a murdered man.' He was then taken out of court, still uttering imprecations against his sentence. On going out of the dock, he shouted 'I'll be damned if I don't have my hat if I never want it again. Its a damned shame of the old .....'

As he was taken to the condemned cell he continued to use the same kind of language but later, when visited by the chaplain, he said that he was sorry for having been so turbulent and explained that he was subject to sudden bouts of passion. He was calm by the time he went to bed and slept a good portion of the night, as he did also on the Sunday night. Over the weekend, he attended devoutly to the instruction of the chaplain, but would make no admission of guilt, apparently believing that, provided he did not confess, he would be reprieved. The clergymen attending him told him that he was deluding himself and begged him to repent. To one he went so far as to admit that his sentence was just but still he persisted in claiming that it was Elizabeth Haigh who had administered the poison. He was visited in the death cell by his family.

He was executed at noon on Monday March 30, 1829. He was only 18. According to the newspapers he was tall and stout for his age and not ill-looking, and there were many women in the crowd which had assembled to watch him die. On the scaffold he prayed a little. As the cap was pulled over his head, the Governor of the Castle took hold of his hand and asked him if he had anything more to say. 'No, Mr Shepherd,' he said, 'I am innocent.' The drop then fell and after some struggling he expired. After hanging for an hour, his body was cut down and taken to the York county hospital for dissection.

Charles Turner and James Twibell, 1831[191]

In 1830 the underground steward of the Duke of Norfolk's Deep Pit colliery[192] was Jonathan Habbershon. At about 8 pm on Tuesday October 5, 1830, having attended to some business in Sheffield, he set off on foot for his home which was next to the mine. His route took him through the Park. As he neared Manor Lane he saw three men he did not recognise, standing together. They were Charles Turner, James Twibell and George Sidney Priestley (nicknamed Putty).

The trio, who were all the worse for drink, had seen Habbershon approaching as they were walking up the Park and had recognised him. Thinking him a good target for

---

[191] Knipe, op. cit., 186-88; *Sheffield Mercury*, October 9 and 16, 1830; March 26, April 2 and April 30, 1831; *Sheffield Independent*, March 26 and 31, April 2 and 30 and May 7, 1831.

robbery, they hurried into nearby Gin Stables Lane, armed themselves with a hedge stake and waited for him to go by. As soon as he had, Priestley ran past him to check whether he had a weapon. Priestley having given him the thumbs up, Turner took up the hedge stake and struck Habbershon a mighty blow to the back of the head, which felled him like an ox. Twibell now ran up and, for good measure, hit the injured man several blows to the head with a flat iron. They then rifled his pockets taking his pocket watch, his money and his keys[193] and ran off leaving him lying insensible in the road with blood pouring out of his head.

About half an hour later Henry Youle, who was walking home from Sheffield to the Intake, saw Habbershon standing on the footpath near Manor Lane. He spoke to him but received only a groan for an answer. At first Youle thought he was drunk but then noticed a pool of blood on the ground and the bloodied hedge stake. 'I've been robbed and beaten by some villains,' said Habbershon in a faint voice. Having found out where he lived Youle, with great difficulty, got him back to his home. As they were nearing Deep Pit, Joseph Hunter, one of Habbershon's neighbours saw them and at once set off to get Mr Ray, the surgeon.[194] As he passed Manor Lane he saw the blood on the ground and the hedge stake. He threw the stake into a field intending to retrieve it on his way back. By the time Mr Ray got to Deep Pit, the injured man was being tended by his wife. On examining his patient, he found that his face was so badly swollen that his eyes were completely shut. He had four large cuts to his head. Of these one could have been caused by the hedge stake but the others had been made by a sharp instrument. In the meantime, Wilde the constable had been informed of the robbery.

As Turner, Twibell and Priestley made their way up the Park that Tuesday night, they were seen. Henry Walker and two companions had passed them on the road and Walker had actually spoken to Twibell, asking him where he had been and getting the reply 'In bed.' John Ashton had also passed them. Walking towards Sheffield, he had first met Habbershon on the road and then, about a minute and a half later, had seen Priestley. When he got a little further on he had seen two other men, one of whom he

---

192 The colliery was at the top of what is now City Road.
193 Disappointingly for the robbers, he had only five half-crowns, four shillings and four pence on him.
194 Of 23, Victoria Street.

had thought was Turner. He had actually called to him by name but he had got no reply and, because it was dark, thought it possible that it was not he.

In the early hours of Wednesday morning Turner and Twibell met Walker again. They asked him if he knew where Butcher was because they had a silver watch to sell. They showed him the watch telling him they wanted twelve shillings for it. He was soon back with the news that Butcher was in the *Green Man*.[195] They set off to see him and, as they were walking, Twibell told Walker that he had already sold his share of the watch to a man called Crony for a pair of trousers. While the pair were at the public house negotiating with Butcher, the constable, who had got wind of what was afoot, came in. He searched Turner but found nothing on him. On Twibell, however, he found a watch, a chain, a seal, two keys, four half crowns and four half-pennies. Asked where he had got the watch, Twibell replied 'From a travelling man at Rotherham races.' The constable took both into custody. The watch was later identified by Mrs Habbershon as her husband's.

On Friday, October 8 Turner and Twibell appeared before Hugh Parker, the magistrate. He took evidence from Youle, Walker, Wilde, and Mrs. Habbershon. Twibell was then taken out of court. In his absence, Turner claimed that on the Tuesday night he had been going part of the way home with Putty when they had met Henry Walker and two others. As Putty's way home was up the Park, he and the others went as far with him as the Sheaf Bridge,[196] where they all agreed to turn back and go to the theatre. As it was too late to go to the full play, they went to the *Three Tuns* at the bottom of Lee Croft. They remained there until nearly 9 o'clock and then went to the theatre.

Twibell was now brought back in. Asked for his whereabouts on the Tuesday night, he said that he had been at the *Three Tuns* until 7.30 and had then gone to the theatre. He had gone to the theatre alone and had not seen Turner or Putty that night. The magistrate remanded both in custody for further examination.

On Saturday October 13, Habbershon being still too ill to attend the Town Hall, Mr Parker went to his home to take his deposition. Before the prisoners were brought in,

---

[195] In Broad Street, Park. Butcher was almost certainly a local fence (receiver of stolen goods).
[196] The Sheaf Bridge linked Dixon Lane with Broad Street.

the magistrate told him to soothe his mind and not be agitated when they came in. Twibell, who had been conveyed to the house in a waterloo,[197] then entered the room. Habbershon, having looked him up and down, said that he could not say whether he was one of his attackers. Twibell was then questioned at length but gave the same answers as at the last examination. He was taken out and Turner was brought in.

Turner proceeded to make a full confession and gave a detailed description of his movements on the Tuesday and the Wednesday morning. He said that he had hit Habbershon with the hedge stake and that Twibell had beaten him about the head with a piece of flat iron. Both prisoners were further remanded.

On the following Friday, they were brought up for final examination along with Priestley, who was now also in custody. They were brought in separately and each was asked whether he wished to say anything about the serious charge against him.

Turner declared that the confession which he had made the previous Saturday had been drawn from him, in consequence of a conversation he had had on morning of that day with Benjamin Jackson, constable Wilde's assistant. Jackson had told him that he could clear himself by turning King's evidence and saying Twibell had struck the first blow. If this allegation was true (and it certainly has the ring of truth about it), it would afford grounds for excluding the confession from evidence at his trial.

When Priestley was questioned, he claimed that he had been with Turner and Twibell on the day of the robbery and in the evening had walked home with them. When they reached Manor Lane they stopped and were debating whether to retrieve some knives which Twibell had left in a quarry hole. As they were talking Habbershon walked by. Twibell said he would fell him like a great sheep, at which Turner picked up a large hedge stake and said 'No, I will do it.' He did not realise at the time that the others intended to rob Habbershon but thought that they were going to attack him because of some grudge. He wanted to go but they made him stay. He gave a description of the robbery which tallied with that given by Turner and said that afterwards the other two made him return to Sheffield with them. The following day he felt sick at the thought of what had been done and, on being asked by his father what ailed him, told him what had happened.

---

[197] A type of coach.

Twibell gave the same sullen answers as he had when last examined, insisting that he knew nothing at all about the robbery.

An additional piece of evidence was brought forward to the effect that the three prisoners had been together within a few minutes of the robbery close to the place where it had been committed.

The evidence being concluded, the magistrates committed all three for trial. They admonished them to employ the time they would spend in prison awaiting trial in reviewing their past lives, warning them that, if a jury should find them guilty, they might afterwards have only a very short time for repentance.

Turner and Twibell's case came on for trial before Mr Justice Parke at the York Spring Assizes 1831.[198] Priestley, as he had no doubt hoped, was admitted King's evidence but, when called into the witness box, he went back on the confession which he had made before the magistrate. It was untrue, he claimed, and had been forced out of him by the constable's telling him if he did not say what he had said he would be transported. The judge ordered him to be taken into custody and directed that a bill of indictment be preferred against him, saying that he would have him tried in the course of the Assize.

Walker and Butcher were called next. Like Priestley, they proved most reluctant witnesses claiming that when they had been examined before the magistrates they had not known what they had said. They did, however, go so far as to admit to having seen the accused, close by the Town Hall, at about 7 pm on the Tuesday night in the company of Priestley, and again in the early hours of the following morning at the *Green Man* offering for sale a watch without seal or chain in which they both claimed a share. Turner's confession was also put in. Neither accused having offered any defence, the judge proceeded to charge the jury who, without hesitation, found both guilty. Parke J immediately put on the black cap and turning to the prisoners said:

> 'Charles Turner and James Twibell, the jury who have just found you guilty have performed their duty to their country and it now remains for me to perform mine. You have been justly convicted and found guilty of a malicious assault committed upon the prosecutor. You were not contented with taking his money but treated him in a cruel manner, beating him dreadfully with a hedge stake and leaving him for dead. Under

---

[198]   Mr Elsley appeared for the prosecution; Mr Cottingham for the defence.

the effects of those blows he still labours and perhaps will continue to do so for the remainder of his life; you therefore deserve the full weight of the law to fall on your heads. It is not my sentence but the sentence of the law that I am about the pass on you: I implore you both, therefore, in the little time you have left to employ it, on your bended knees, in obtaining the pardon from God Almighty which you cannot hope for here; and may God have mercy on your souls. The sentence of the law is that you be conveyed from this place to the place from whence you came and from thence to the place of execution where you are to be hung by the neck till you are dead.'

During the passing of the sentence both men were 'drowned in tears and earnestly begged for mercy.'

On Saturday March 26, 1831 Priestley took his trial.[199] The record of his examination before the magistrates was put in, in which he had stated that he saw Turner and Twibell beat the prosecutor and rob him. Several witnesses were called to prove that Priestley was near the spot at about the time the outrage was committed but, owing to the darkness of the night, none of them could be positive as to his person. In his defence, the prisoner said that his declarations before the magistrates were true and explained his conduct on Thursday by saying that the prisoners' friends had threatened him if he appeared against them, and that the witness Butcher 'had ever held out threats to him since the Assizes began.' Butcher was recalled and insisted that Priestley's accusation was false. The judge, thinking that it was, in fact, probably true, summed up for an acquittal and the jury duly brought in a verdict of not guilty.[200]

In Sheffield, meanwhile, attempts were being made to try and secure a reprieve for the two condemned. On Sunday April 24, 1831, a petition asking that mercy be extended to them was forwarded to Lord Melbourne, the Home Secretary. He replied by return of post. 'There was no feature in their cases that would warrant his recommending them to the Mercy of the Sovereign.' One of those who wanted their lives saved was Habbershon and they wrote to him from the condemned cell, expressing their gratitude:

> 'We return to you grateful thanks for your kindness that you have bestowed upon us of [trying to get] our lives spared but we do not expect it. We are preparing for another world and hope you will forgive us for what you have had from us. We should never have done the crime we are charged with if we had not been intoxicated. We shall be executed on

---

[199] Mr. Elsley and Mr Wortley prosecuted. Mr Cottingham appeared for Priestley.
[200] The *Sheffield Mercury*, April 2, 1831 reported 'The prisoner appeared a poor illiterate lad, completely under the control of the two convicted parties.' Like them he was 19 years of age.

Saturday next. You must let my father know that I have written to you and hope we shall meet in heaven where sorrow never comes.'

As the letter predicted, they were hanged at noon on Saturday April 30, 1831. On appearing on the drop they gazed in wonderment at the large crowd. After joining in earnestly with the chaplain's prayers they were placed beneath the beam still praying fervently. The hoods were placed over their faces and the nooses around their necks, then the drop fell 'and they were no more.'

After hanging for the usual time, the bodies were cut down and handed over to their friends. They were taken back to a house in the Park on Sunday night and were interred in the Parish Churchyard on the Wednesday morning. Thousands of persons attended the interment, most of them women.

On April 30 the *Sheffield Independent* reported that after the bodies had been brought back to Sheffield, their friends had, for the next two days, charged the public money to see them. The price of admission varied according to the visitor's means. The following week it published a partial retraction:

> The paper had been credibly informed that during the days that Turner's body lay in his relatives' house in the Park no such exhibition took place and that a few donations which were voluntarily made were for the purpose of obtaining for the corpse a decent burial.

Turner and Twibell were both just 19 years of age.

Thomas Rodgers, 1834 [201]

Of this 32-year-old little is known except that he was a labourer. He was convicted at the York Spring Assizes, 1834 of committing buggery with George Bennett, a fellow workman. He had apparently confessed his crime to his employer and it was this confession which was the principal evidence against him at his trial. Baron Alderson, passing sentence of death, told him that the offence of which he had been convicted:

---

[201]   Knipe, op. cit., pp. 191-92; *Sheffield Mercury*, April 5, 1834; other reports are to be found in the *Sheffield Independent*, February 1 and March 29, 1834; *Hull Rockingham*, March 2, 1834, *Hull Packet*, April 4, 1834. *Hull Advertiser*, April 4, 1834 and *The Times* April 29, 1834.

'was one from which human nature shuddered and from the contemplation of which the mind shrank back with horror. It was one which struck at the root of the propagation of society and was one prohibited by the laws both of God and man and he stood there convicted of having given vent to an unbridled lust, a melancholy spectacle to teach men to ask for God's holy spirit to keep their thoughts from evil' [202]

The judge, who according to newspaper reports was obviously distressed,[203] said that he sincerely regretted that it had fallen to his lot to pass upon him the awful sentence of the law. He made it plain that he intended to leave him for execution and urged him to seek the mercy of the Almighty. Rodgers, who affected disinterest whilst sentence was being passed, left the dock without saying a word.

Following conviction he was attended by a number of clergy, including the prison chaplain, who together succeeded in bringing him to a state of repentance. On the Thursday before he was to hang he was present in the prison chapel to hear the condemned sermon preached,[204] and on the Friday he took his leave of his brother and sister in law.

He was hanged on Saturday April 16, 1834. By 7 am that day the scaffold had been erected and spectators were already beginning to gather in front of it. By 11 am Castle Green and the streets leading to it resembled a fair, with a continual stream of men, women and children passing through, all heading for the Drop. Many of the crowd were from Leeds and the West Riding, but the villages of the North and East Ridings had also contributed their quota. At 11.30, Rodgers, Morrow and Cook, who were all to hang at noon, were pinioned. A few minutes before midday they were taken from their cells across the low grates yard, under the chapel, through the half moon yard and along the passage leading to the drop. As they stepped out onto the platform the huge crowd [205] fell silent. Prayers were offered by the chaplain in which the condemned men joined with great earnestness. Rodgers and Morrow acknowledged the justice of their sentences but Cook did not. The executioner now took over. The three men were

---

[202] *Sheffield Mercury*

[203] The *Hull Advertiser*, April 29, 1834 describes him as 'greatly affected'; the *Hull Rockingham* March 29, 1839 speaks of his displaying 'considerable emotion.'

[204] The preacher, the Rev J Crosby, took as his text *Isaiah*, 55 v. 6 ' Seek ye the Lord that he may be found.'

[205] The *Sheffield Mercury*, May 3, 1834 reported that the crowd was not less than 6,000. Some of the spectators had gathered across the river to watch the proceedings from there.

placed under the beam with Morrow in the centre, Cook to his left and Rodgers on his right. Rodgers was the first to have the white cap drawn over his head and had to wait while the hangmen adjusted the ropes on the necks of his two companions. The delay caused him to become very agitated but then the drop fell. He was the first to expire but appeared to suffer greatly as did Cook and Morrow, who were both convulsed, especially the latter who seemed to die in great agony.[206] As soon as they were all dead the crowd dispersed and, for some time after, the surrounding streets were 'choked with people as far as the eye could see.'

Cook and Rodgers were both buried in a single grave in the church-yard of St Mary, Castlegate.

William Allott, 1835 [207]

In the 1830s Sheffield got its milk from outlying farms like that of Martha Hardwick at Upper Heeley. Living on that small farm in early 1834 were three people, Martha herself, William Allott, her cohabitee and 12-year-old milk boy, Joseph Wolstenholme. Allott, who called himself farm manager, was a domineering man and Martha seems to have been very much under this thumb. He beat her when the fancy took him which it often did when he was in drink. The milk lad had seen him knock her down more than once and she was forever complaining of his ill-treatment.

A little before seven o'clock on the morning of Tuesday September 9 Allott called on his neighbours, the Gillotts, and asked for and was given a pint of water. He drank it down greedily. 'That will sober me,' he said. 'I'm off to Sheffield to take out a warrant against my sister. She's taken a sovereign from my box locker.' An hour later he and the lad set off for town on the milk cart. When they got there, Allott went straight to the Town Hall, took out the summons and immediately repaired to the public house next door.[208] He was still there drinking at 3 pm when Wolstenholme popped his head round the door to tell him that he had to be setting off back. Allott, who still had a

---

[206] The order of the deaths is taken from the *Sheffield Mercury* but it may be wrong. According to the report in the *York Herald* Cook died first and did not suffer, then Rodgers and then Morrow.

[207] Knipe, op. cit., p. 192; *The Times*, April 4 and 6, 1835; *Sheffield Mercury*, April 11, 1835 and *York Herald*, April 11, 1835.

[208] *The Black Rock*, 17, Castle Street.

thirst on him, let him go. By 4 pm the boy was back at the farm. He fetched the cows from the field and, after they had been milked, chatted briefly with Martha before setting off for Sheffield with the next delivery.

By the time he returned it was getting on for 7 pm. As he was unloading the milk barrels, Martha appeared carrying a can of water. 'I'm going to take the cows up the field, once I've done this' he told her. 'Alright' she said. Once he had finished his tasks, he went to play in the fields near the *Waggon and Horses* public house.

Allott, meanwhile, had been making his way back from Sheffield on foot. At about 7:30 he was in Sleigh Bush's grocer's shop in Bramall Lane. By now it was already dark. Shortly after, his neighbour Joseph Cartwright caught up with him. As they walked together, they reminisced about their younger days when Cartwright had been an apprentice and Allott in service. Then Allott, who was obviously the worse for drink, suddenly launched into a diatribe against his sister. When they reached the bridge at the end of Bramall Lane, he suggested they cut across the fields, but Cartwright said he preferred to stick to the road and did. It was by now around 7:40 pm and Allott was just a couple of fields from home.

Just before 8 pm, Mrs Gillott was standing talking to Martha Greenwood, when she saw Allott coming across her garden. She shouted to him that it wasn't a road. He replied that he had thought Martha Greenwood was his sister and he asked if she had seen his sister. He then went into his own house. He was wearing a frock coat, breeches and gaiters and appeared tipsy.

Minutes later two young girls, Elizabeth Burley and Mary Muscroft, were passing the Gillotts' house when they heard someone shout out 'He's killing me!' and then 'Oh dear!' The shouts appeared to come from next door. Mary ran and told her mother but she, having often heard rowing between Allott and Martha in the past, thought nothing of it. At around the same time George Rainey, a file forger who lived thirty yards from the Martha's farmhouse, was at work in his shop when he heard a scream. He went to the door and looked across but, hearing nothing more, went back inside. A few minutes later there was another scream. This time he walked down the side of his workshop to a place from which he had a clear view of the Hardwick farm. As he listened he could hear Allott's voice cursing and swearing as if in a passion, a woman asking 'What have

I done amiss, William?' and Allott shouting that she was a whore and was robbing him every day. Rainey went back to his work; as he later explained, arguments between the couple were so common that he thought no more of it.

About ten minutes later Allott appeared at the Gillotts' buttery window. 'Have you a candle? Our mistress is drunk' he asked Mrs Gillott. 'Very likely she is drunk with water, if she is,' she replied, handing him a taper.

Shortly afterwards, the milk lad arrived back from playing. He at once noticed blood on the kitchen floor. He went into the parlour where he found Allott, his clothes all bloody, in the act of lifting Martha onto the bed.

'What hast thou been doing to get our mistress knocked on the head?' Allott asked.

'She was well and hearty when I took the cows to the field.'

'How long have you been away?'

'About half an hour.'

'As I was walking up the field two men ran from the house. I tried to jump over a wall to cut them off but pulled my shoe to pieces doing so,' Allott explained, turning to where Martha was lying.

She was a sorry sight: covered in blood, her hair ruffled, her cap ripped off and her clothes torn from her back. She could not get up and was calling out 'Help me! Come here!' and wiping blood off her face. 'Who has done this?' Allott asked her. 'Oh, what am I to do?' she cried, leaving his question unanswered. He went for water, gave her some on a spoon and sprinkled the rest on her face. He then took off his coat and gaiters and put them at the top of the stairs. 'I got blood on them helping Martha, See thee,' he said, bringing a pair of shoes out from the pantry, 'I'll show thee my shoes. I rent the seam in getting over the wall.' The lad's sharp eyes noticed that, as well as being torn, they had blood and hair on them. After pondering some time, Allott said 'We are like to have some help' and asked the boy to go fetch a doctor. 'I am too afraid,' he answered.

'Then we'll both go.'

By now it was a good half-hour since Wolstenholme had arrived back at the farm and the alarm still had not been not raised.

They set off for the house of Boler, the constable. He was not in but caught up with them near Hannah Thompson's house. He asked why they had called on him. 'Somebody has given our mistress something and made her fresh and almost murdered her,' Allott told him.

'Murdered her?'

'Aye, I saw two men run from our house across Burgy Gillott's[209] garden and I jumped over and followed them but I could not catch them.' Allott added that he was on his way to Hannah Thompson's to ask her to come and tend to Martha.

Boler went straight to the farm and got there ahead of Allott. The door was open and, lying on a bed in the parlour, covered in blood and apparently insensible was Martha. Her clothes had been torn off her, leaving her left arm tangled in her gown. The constable noticed that the gown had several holes in it. 'Who has done this?' he asked. 'Help me! Help me!' was all she answered. Allott now arrived and asked Boler to fetch a doctor. 'You must go,' said the officer. Allott said that he would go for Mr Wright[210] since he was the nearest in Sheffield. 'Wait at the surgery until I get there,' Boler instructed.

At 10 o'clock Martha died. The constable now took the opportunity to make a thorough search of the house. On the parlour floor he found a two-pronged table fork which was bloody and had been wiped. The cloth used to wipe it was lying nearby on a table. There was a lot of blood on the back and the arm of the sofa and on the floor. At the foot of the bed on which the body lay were a broken chair, a smashed pot[211] and a corn riddle with blood on it. There was also blood on the kitchen floor, with a trail leading from kitchen to parlour. Both downstairs rooms were in a state of complete disarray with furniture overturned.

Allott got to Mr. Wright's at about 10.30. Wright's pupil, Hugh Mellor, answered the door. 'The doctor's not in,' he told him.

'Well, will you come and see a person called Hardwick who lives at the top of Upper Heeley and is dangerously ill?

---

[209] Mrs Gillot's first name was Burgoyne.
[210] Probably James Wright of 93, Norfolk Street.
[211] A panshion is how it is described in press reports.

'What is wrong with her?'

'Some people have tried to murder her. She is cut all over. I found her laid down in a corner of the house and thinking her drunk and said 'Martha, I am surprised as you should do so as to get fresh.' I carried her into the next room and laid her down by the side of a corn bin, and then took no further notice of her for an hour, thinking she was simply tipsy; but then I looked for a candle and, when I found one and saw what state she was in, I raised the alarm and went for the constable.'

Realising that the case was serious, Mellor went to fetch Mr Wright. When Wright got to the farm, Martha had been dead for over an hour. Boler locked up the house and returned with him to his surgery where Allott was waiting. 'Is she dead?' he asked. 'Yes,' replied Boler.

'I am innocent and have not injured her.'

'I believe you killed her.'

'Surely, you don't think so. I hope you have a better opinion of me.'

Boler told him that he must go with him to the Town Hall. 'Surely not' said Allott. Boler told him he must. He tried to handcuff him but the cuffs were too small. When they got to the Town Hall, Boler handed him over to Cooper, the gaoler, who searched him and put him in a cell. He had 4s 4½d on him. Cooper noticed that his shirt-sleeves were bloody and that he had spots of blood on his chin. The next morning he brought him a cup of coffee and asked how he was. 'Middling' was the reply. 'What do you think of the affair?' Allott asked him. 'Is it serious?'

'Very serious.'

'Supposing they can prove it against me, they will not hang me till March.'

'If you have anything on your mind, I would recommend you to make your peace with God as soon as possible,' Cooper advised.

'I am as innocent as you are. I found her on the floor and took her into the parlour, which was the cause of the blood on me.'

By 7 o'clock that morning Boler was back at the farm, looking for footprints or other evidence of persons having run away from it. He found none; the garden was well stocked with potatoes but the tops of the plants were undisturbed. Near the top of Gillotts' garden he found the impression of the heel of a man's shoe but the mark was pointing towards, not away from, Hardwick's. He also examined the wall, which separated the two properties, but found no marks either near to it or on it. He went inside the house. From upstairs he recovered Allott's bloodied frock coat (he was already in possession of the bloodied gaiters which had been found behind the sofa the previous evening and handed to him then). Downstairs he found a blue apron, which looked as though it had been used for wiping up blood.

A post-mortem was performed by Mr Wright. He found, on external examination, that both eyes were bruised and swollen and one of them closed, the nose was broken; the upper lip had been penetrated by a sharp object, like the prong of a fork, which had gone into the gum and the face was scratched and bloody; there was bruising to the back, an abrasion to the knee and an oblique fracture of the left arm, the bones of which had been penetrated by a sharp instrument; the brain was congested and there were fractures of the 6th and 7th left ribs and the 7th right rib and lacerations to the liver and left kidney. There was no liquor in the stomach. The surgeon thought that the wound to the lip might have been caused by the fork found at the house, but that some heavier instrument had been used to inflict the injury to the arm. That her death had been caused by the injuries she had received was beyond doubt.

On the Tuesday an inquest was held before the coroner, Thomas Badger, at the *Waggon and Horses* and continued on the Wednesday in the petty sessions court at the Town Hall. On the Wednesday, after the taking of the evidence had been completed, Allott was brought in and the depositions read to him. He stood the whole of the time looking at the table in front of him, seldom raising his eyes. After being cautioned he made the following statement:

'I was at Sheffield at 8 o'clock. I can't say any more, only that I found her in the house when I got in. I took her into the parlour before I went to George Gillott's to fetch a candle. I put her on the bed. I fell over a chopping box or a great tub. I never touched her but carried her into the parlour. I believe I was at Mr Sleigh Bush's shop in Bramall Lane the last place. It was then I think a little after 8 o'clock. When a man is fresh he cannot exactly recall what time it was. I don't know anything more. I have no witnesses I wish you to examine. Only the little lad came into the house. I was not sober.'

The coroner then summed up the evidence and, after a short retirement, the jury brought in a verdict of murder against Allott. He was immediately committed to York. By now it was 11 pm.

On the way to York, Allott complained to Cooper that it was a pity that a man like him should be chained hand and foot when he was innocent of the crime. He had no reason to hurt her, poor thing. She had cooked him a supper of beef steaks and kidney beans and left it covered up on the oven. If he did it, he was drunk and soft and did not know what he was doing. At the trial Boler would confirm that he had found a plate of steak and potatoes on the oven top.

The local press had no doubt who had done the deed, the *Sheffield Mercury* commenting that 'the horrible affair added another instance to the fatal results of intemperance.'

Allott was tried at York Spring Assizes in March 1835 before Baron Alderson.[212] The jury convicted without retiring. After sentence of death had been passed, insisting that he was innocent, he begged that his body be given to his father and friends. The judge told him that he had no power to grant his request and asked him rather to consider the interests of his soul. After he had been taken from the dock, he was found to be in possession of a large knife, which he had presumably been intending to use to kill himself.

He was hanged at 11 am on April 6, 1835 along with two other murderers, Ursula Lofthouse and Joseph Heeley. A large crowd had gathered in front of the drop. Many of the spectators, believing that the execution was to take place at 8 had been waiting for nearly five hours.[213] On the scaffold Allott protested his innocence to the last but it was noticed that he prayed as fervently as his two companions, who had both acknowledged their guilt. He was the first to step onto the platform and, on doing so, he 'surveyed the crowd with a look of apparent calmness tinged with fear.' The nooses having been adjusted all three were turned off. Heeley was convulsed for some minutes but Allott and Lofthouse, who was in the middle, appeared to die almost

---

[212] Mr Baines and Mr Wortley conducted the prosecution. Allott was defended by Sir Gregory Lewin.
[213] It was reported in the *Sheffield Independent* that pickpockets had been working the crowd assembled to watch the execution.

instantaneously. All three bodies were buried within the castle precincts. Allott was 35 years old.

Charles Batty, 1836 [214]

In summer 1835 ex- soldier Charles Batty took up with Elizabeth Brown and soon they were living together in a garret in Cush Yard, Mill Sands. Money was not plentiful and what little they had too often went on drink. By September their lack of money was becoming acute and they were constantly quarrelling. Sunday 13th was particularly miserable. A single potato was the only food they had all day. At 9 o'clock Elizabeth decided to go to bed. Batty followed her up but, instead of getting into bed, seated himself in front of the fire and smoked a pipe. His thoughts soon turned to food. 'What is there for tomorrow's dinner?' he enquired 'I'd like milk and potatoes and is there any tobacco?' 'Where am I to get it from? I have no money,' was Elizabeth's sharp reply. Batty turned on her angrily. 'I'll be independent of you and everyone,' he told her, snuffing out the candle. 'Why have you put the candle out when you aren't undressed?' she asked. Hoping, no doubt, to shut her up he made to re-light it. 'Never mind lighting it again, we shall not be so sure to get another,' she told him. At this he completely lost his temper and went for her throat. At first she thought he had merely grabbed it but then she saw blood running down her arm. She clambered out of bed only for Batty to seize her by the hair and start pulling her round the room by it. 'Murder' she screamed. Batty warned her to make less noise or it would be the worse for her. At this point she broke free and ran to the top of the stairs. He was on her at once and, taking hold of her, lifted her up and threw her over the banister rail, shouting 'There you bloody go.' She fell to the bottom of the staircase landing against the street door.

The commotion brought Eaton, their landlord, running from his house in nearby Mill Lane. He found Elizabeth lying on the ground with her throat cut. He took her to his

---

[214] Knipe, op. cit., p. 197; *Sheffield Independent*, March 12, 1836, *The Times*, April 5 1836.

house and then returned to Cush Yard and climbed up to the garret. There he found Batty bandaging his thumb. He asked for a pin to fasten the bandage but Eaton would not give him one, saying he had murdered Elizabeth Brown. Batty was detained and handed over to the constable. You face a very serious charge the officer told him. 'I know that,' he replied 'I ought to have finished her long ago. She's pawned all my clothes.' What did you cut her with?' he was asked. 'With a razor,' he said. While he was being spoken to his room was being searched and minutes later a man named Stephenson emerged and handed over to the constable a bloody razor which he had found in the garret grate covered in ashes. Batty was then taken away, complaining that he had cut his thumb and insisting that he was not sorry for what he had done.

In the meantime, surgeon William Jackson[215] had been sent for. When he arrived he found Elizabeth Brown sitting in a chair, with three people pressing towels to a cut to her throat. The cut, which started at the right ear and which was 4½ inches long and, at one point, 1½ inches deep, had severed four arteries and come within an ace of severing her wind pipe. There was also a cut to her neck, a cut to her thumb, cuts to her back and superficial cuts and bruising to her breast. It took him three hours to repair the damage to the blood vessels of the neck and to stitch the cut. He thought her in extreme danger and did not expect her to survive his surgery. Astonishingly she did.[216]

On March 7, 1836 Batty stood trial at York Spring Assizes on an indictment charging him with cutting and wounding Elizabeth Brown with intent to murder her.[217] When Brown gave her evidence Batty, who had no counsel, put to her in cross-examination that he had given her money on the Friday and Saturday, which she had spent on drink. She denied this, saying that she had used it to get clothes out of pawn and repay a debt. She agreed that all they had had to eat on the Sunday was one potato between them. In answer to questions from the judge, Mr Baron Parke, she said she had never known the prisoner to be deranged in his mind. He had threatened her twice before and had on one occasion taken a razor to her.

---

[215] William Jackson of 18, Bank Street.
[216] In the 1830s all that was available to deaden pain was alcohol. It was not until the following decade that surgeons began to use nitrous oxide (1844), ether (1844) and chloroform (1846) to induce anaesthesia.
[217] Mr Milner and Mr. Parker were counsel for the prosecution. Batty was undefended.

At the close of the Crown case, Batty was asked what he had to say in his defence. He told the jury that when he first met Elizabeth Brown he lived in Spring Street. She was continually after him and at last he fetched his clothes from his lodgings; he had lived with her for four months and gave her twelve shillings a week, with the exception of the last when he was out of work. He sold his watch on the Friday and gave her seven shillings of the money he got for it. When he came back in the evening he found her in liquor. He gave her two shillings more on the Saturday but, when he came home that evening, there was nothing for him to eat. He asked her whether or not she had bought anything and she said 'No. I'll make you sup sorrow by the spoonful. You shall be hanged or transported for my sake.' He took the keys of his box from her and when he opened it found that all his clothes had been pawned. He asked her the reason and she replied 'I'll pawn you, if you are not off.' He got up on Sunday morning and found there was no breakfast. He got two cups of tea and a bit of dry bread from the man who lived below. With trouble and grief and uneasiness he began drinking. He got two six-pennyworths of rum and nine or ten pints of ale during the day. He did not know how he had got home but the next morning found himself in prison. He said he had been seven years and five months in His Majesty's service and trusted that his Lordship and the jury would be merciful to him.

Constable Bland was immediately recalled and asked whether Batty had been displaying signs of intoxication on arrest. 'No,' he replied 'he was sober.'[218]

The judge then charged the jury who, after a few minutes consultation, brought back a verdict of guilty. The judge proceeded immediately to pass sentence. The verdict of the jury, he said, placed him in the unhappy position of telling the prisoner that he must suffer an ignominious death upon the scaffold. He had most unquestionably tried to murder the woman with whom he had lived in a state of misery... His mind had, no doubt, been exasperated against her from causes to which her conduct had contributed, but which formed no excuse for him. It was utterly impossible that any other sentence could be pronounced than would have been if death had ensued. He trusted that the remaining hours, which the prisoner had to live, would be spent in an endeavour to repent of the crime which he had committed and that his awful death would be a warning to others and prevent their indulging in such fatal passions. The sentence was that he be taken from hence to the place whence he came and then to the place of execution there to be hanged by the neck until he was dead. Batty, who appeared unmoved, was then taken from the dock.

He was executed on Saturday April 2, 1836. On the scaffold he appeared firm but resigned to his fate. After spending a short time in prayer he gave himself up to the hands of the hangman. He was one of the last men to be hanged in England for attempted murder. He was buried in the churchyard of St Mary, Castlegate. He was 28 years old.

Thomas Williams, 1837 [219]

In January 1837 George Moore, who had a small factory in Silver Street Head, Sheffield set on Thomas Williams as a basket maker. Williams, who was a heavy drinker, proved a less than satisfactory workman, regularly taking days off to go on drinking sprees. In March, Moore lost patience, gave him two weeks' notice and set on Thomas Froggatt in his stead. But then he relented and agreed to keep him on. The incident left Williams with a grudge against Froggatt, whom he regarded as having tried to steal his job. It certainly did not lead to any mending of his ways: in the week beginning Monday March 13, rather than turn up for work, Moore went drinking in town.

Friday, March 17 was no different. Having spent the morning boozing, at 1 o'clock he went to the Fargate lodgings of a basket maker, called Buggins, and asked him to come for a drink. Buggins agreed and the two of them went to the *Black Swan* [220] where they ordered ale. Williams said he had something to tell Buggins and suggested that they sit down. When they were seated, he told him 'I have a point in view and, if I can accomplish it, I will make you a present of my shears as I shall never use them again. You must keep them for my sake.' Pressed for an explanation, he said he meant

[218] Elizabeth Brown was also recalled on the point. She too was adamant that Batty was not in drink.
[219] Knipe, op. cit., 197-98; *Sheffield Independent*, April 8 (inquest), July 8 and 22, 1837; *The Times* July 17 and August 16, 1837; *York Herald*, August 12, 1837.
[220] In Fargate.

to kill Froggatt and would mash his brains out that night. 'You can't think of doing so.' Buggins protested. 'You can't be so cruel.' 'I can,' insisted Williams, adding that it concerned work and he would mash Froggatt's brains out.

The pair went on to *Linley's*, a public house near Moore's workshop, where they called for a pint of beer. Williams went across to the workshop but came back, complaining that he could not find his shears although his other tools were there. Buggins suggested his wife might have them. 'No,' said Williams, 'I don't think she has' and went back to look again. He returned saying he still hadn't found them. He entered the workshop for a third time and went over to the window, as if looking for his tools. Froggatt was sitting nearby with his back to him. Williams, by now only feet away, suddenly produced a billhook and struck him a violent blow on the side of the head, driving the weapon into the skull with such force that he had great difficulty pulling it out. Having freed it, he struck Froggatt a second time shouting 'Damn him, I will finish him.' All this had been witnessed by a workman called Jeffries who, terrified, rushed out in to the street and shouted for people to come and help.

Minutes later Williams emerged, went straight into *Linley's* and announced to the assembled company 'I've done it.' 'What have you done?' asked Buggins. 'I've killed old Frog,' was the reply. Jeffries then came in and, pointing to Williams, said 'He's killed old Froggatt.' Buggins immediately went over to the workshop where he saw Froggatt lying insensible on the floor, with blood oozing from two large wounds in his head. A billhook covered in blood lay nearby. He returned to *Linley's* and said to Williams 'Tom, you have not killed him.' 'If I thought I had not, I'd have given him another chop' was the belligerent reply. 'Tom, they'll hang you as sure as you are born' warned Buggins. Williams said he did not give a damn and that they might hang him there and then if Froggatt was dead.

Buggins now went out into the street again and was in time to see Froggatt carried down from the shop and put into a cart which was to take him to the Infirmary. On arrival at hospital he was examined and found to have a six-inch cut which ran from the crown of the head to the middle of his left temple, exposing the skull in two places. The wound was dressed and Froggatt admitted to one of the wards.

As Froggatt was being taken to hospital, Williams set off for the *Windsor Castle* [221] and it was there that Waterfall, the constable, found him. After some prevarication, he admitted that he had attacked Froggatt. Told he was under arrest, he agreed to go with the officer and drank off his ale, saying 'If he dies, I'll be satisfied. If not, I'll be sorry.' Waterfall cautioned him against saying anything more. Williams took no notice and continued to talk as they made their way to the Town Hall: 'Damn, if he dies it will be a good thing for the trade. He was a damned rascal. He wanted to take my bread off my trencher and if I have not killed him it is a pity. If I have killed him the trade will have the benefit of it. I care nothing for myself but, if I have not killed him and am to suffer for it, I shall be sorry.' Froggatt lingered on until April 5.

On March 25 Mr Brownall, the magistrate, took his deposition at the hospital with Williams present. In that deposition, he said he had known Williams ten years and that he was friendly with him when he went to Moore's. They had had some snagging but no quarrel. He had been at work most of last week but Williams had been on the drinking tack. On the Friday afternoon he was working in the shop with Jeffries when Williams came in looking for his shears. Not finding them, he went out again but soon returned and came and stood by the window. Williams then said 'Here goes' and struck him a heavy blow to the head. He remembered little more and did not know why Williams had struck him. Williams declined to ask Froggatt any questions but merely shook hands with him.

A post-mortem performed by Mr Jackson, a surgeon at the Infirmary, established that the blow which caused the wound had fractured the skull in two places and had also penetrated the brain at one point to a depth of about an inch, the brain tissue in this area being bloody and inflamed. There were two other wounds on the left side of the skull but neither of these had penetrated the skull. The surgeon was in no doubt that the wound to the head was the cause of Froggatt's death, for in all other respects he was in good health.

On March 7, an inquest was held before Thomas Badger, the county coroner. After the evidence of the surgeon and the eye-witnesses had been taken, Williams was brought in and their depositions were read to him. He said he had no witnesses to call

---

[221] In Silver Street.

and did not wish to say anything. He told the coroner that some of the witnesses had spoken the truth, but he could not speak to the whole of them at present. The coroner summed up briefly and the jury having returned a verdict of murder he was committed for trial.

He was tried before Mr Justice Coltman at the summer Assizes, 1837.[222] His counsel, Mr Bliss, sought to persuade the jury that, at the time of the attack, his client was suffering from insanity 'irritated by drink.' But the evidence was against him, Jeffries and Buggins both being adamant that, although intoxicated, Williams was in perfect possession of his faculties and well knew what he was doing. The judge summed up the evidence with minute particularity, leaving it to the jury to say whether insanity was made out. They having brought back the inevitable verdict, the judge put on the black cap and passed sentence of death. He told Williams that he could leave him no hope of mercy. When his lordship said 'May the lord have mercy on your soul' Williams closed his eyes and said very fervently 'Amen,' as did many in the public gallery.

He was executed at noon on Saturday August 12, 1837. On the scaffold he prayed with great fervour and then turned and addressed the crowd:

> 'Fellow men you are come to witness a spectacle of intemperance, an awful scene; I hope this will make a lasting impression upon every soul before me. A man in the prime of his life, 30 years of age, cut off through this diabolical crime of intemperance. Is there a drunkard before me? Yes, I see many. Let him go home and be so no more. Is there a liar? Let him speak the truth for the future and turn to God with a full purpose of heart. I have to inform you that I am leaving a grateful partner behind me, one that is walking in the commandments of the Lord and one that delights in her God; therefore I hope I shall meet her in heaven. I have also not a doubt of my acceptance with that God whom I am going to stand before. Oh! That everyone of you may seek the Lord because He may be found. May you turn to him and God Almighty grant that I may meet you all in the Kingdom of Heaven.'

The bolt was drawn and after a short struggle he died. His body was buried within the precincts of the prison. The crowd at the execution was not large but amongst them there was a great proportion of females some with children in their arms.

Williams left a widow and five children.

---

[222] The prosecution was conducted by Mr Dundas and Mr. Wortley.

Robert Nall, 1842 [223]

Robert Nall married his wife Mary in 1833. The marriage proved an unhappy one and, during the next eight years, they travelled the country separating on at least seven occasions. In January 1841 they parted again. By October, Nall wanted Mary back and several times that month turned up at her mother's house where she was lodging. Each time he tried to persuade her to return to him, but she would not. So persistent was he and so abusive when rebuffed that eventually she took out a summons against him. In the early hours of Sunday October 27 he turned up again and asked Banks, who owned the house, to send his wife out. Banks told him if he came at a proper hour he should see her. At this, he went away, saying he would be back at 9 am, which he was. This time he managed to see to his wife.

'I don't want to talk to you' she told him.'

'I am going out of town. Will you foot a pair of stockings for me?'

'No. Go and do the best for thyself.'

'Then I mean to tell thee what I mean to do. Thou must prepare thyself for a coffin tomorrow morning for I mean to stick thee.'

Some time after this he bumped into his sister-in-law, Ann Hall, in the street. She begged him not to behave so badly to his wife and said that she had heard that he had told his wife that he would prepare her for a coffin. That's all nonsense, he replied but on November 3 he was round at her house at Bridge Houses, telling her to tell Mary that he was going to do what he had threatened and she, Mary, knew that when he said a thing he meant it. They would not have much more trouble, for he intended to have a free ride to York.

Despite his threats, he, in fact, did nothing and in late November he and Mary became reconciled.

At about 9:30 pm on November 27 they turned up at the *Hull Beer and Eating House* in the Wicker and asked James Shaw, the manager, for a bed for the night. They had a meal and seemed quite friendly. They went to bed at quarter to eleven and got up at

---

[223] Knipe, op. cit., p. 202; *The Times*, March 19, 1842; *Sheffield Independent*, March 19 and April 16, 1842.

eleven the next morning. They dined at midday and at about 2 o'clock Mary went out, saying she was going to her mother's to wash and change her dress. While she was away, Nall told Shaw that the two of them had been parted about nine months but were going to get together again. They had lived in a house with her mother but in a fortnight they would move to a house of their own. When his wife returned she said her mother was very unwilling that she should return to him. At 5 o'clock they both left. They were quite sober, neither had had more than three pints and Nall appeared quite rational. During their stay at the eating house, he had been as attentive to his wife as if they were newly weds and seemed very happy at the idea of living with her again.

Three hours later they turned up at the house of Nall's sister, Lucy, in Bee Hive Lane[224] and asked for a room for the night. Both were in drink, with Nall the worse affected. At first she refused to let them stop but then relented. They appeared on friendly terms and retired to bed at quarter to nine. The sister then went out, locking the house door behind her, and visited her friend, Mrs Stones, in Carver Street. When she got back at about midnight her brother was standing in front of the fire. She asked him where Mary was. He replied he had been ill-using her and feared he had killed her. She asked him to stop while she got her brother Alfred, who lived about a mile away at Andrew Street in the Nursery, and then went out, locking the door.

Having roused Alfred, she returned to her house accompanied by him, by Mrs Stone and by a watchman called Macklin. Once inside, she lit a candle and they all went upstairs. There they found Nall in bed with his wife. Alfred said to him 'Oh dear, Bob what hasta been doing?' 'I don't know,' he replied. The watchman repeated the question and this time Nall answered that he had murdered his wife with a knife. He got out of bed and handed over a pocket-knife. Before leaving the room he kissed his wife's body. Soon afterwards they all set off for the police office. On the way Nall told Macklin that he should be hung for her, but she would never go with another man any more. He appeared rational, sober, and sorry for what he had done. He pulled up his shirt and showed Macklin where he had tried to stab himself, but said that it had hurt and that he could not do it. He had also tried to hang himself with a handkerchief, but it

---

[224] Off Glossop Road close by the *Bee Hive* public house.

broke.

At about 4 am he was spoken to at the Town Hall by Raynor, the chief officer of police.[225] He told Raynor that he had been on Saturday night and the best part of Sunday with his wife at a beer-house on the Wicker. After leaving there, they had had spirits, ale, beef and bread at several places. They then went to Lucy Nall's for a bed for the night and retired at about 9 o'clock. After some time, they had words and his wife said she wished she had not come to him again. He had replied 'Thou wants to go with that chap again' (meaning a man called Hibbert). She answered that she would go where she liked and with whom she liked. He said 'Why does thou say so? Let us be comfortable.' 'Go to hell with thee' was her reply. At this he got out of bed, took a knife out of his trouser pocket and stabbed her with it. She said 'Oh Bob! Thou's killed me. Kiss me.' He did and got into bed with her and lay with her till 11 o'clock when his sister returned. He told his sister what he had done and then went back and lay with his wife till the watchman came.

A surgeon was called to the house after Nall had been taken away. On examining the body he found five wounds; there were superficial wounds to the neck, hand and shoulder, but the mortal wound was under the left breast. This was nearly 4" deep and had passed through the liver into the stomach.

On Tuesday November 30 an inquest was held at the *Bee Hive* public house[226] at which Nall gave the same account as he had to Raynor in the cells. He was committed for trial, the coroner telling him that 'he never knew a more deliberate and wicked act of murder.'[227] His case came on at the Spring Assizes 1842 before Mr Justice Coltman. His only hope of an acquittal lay in convincing the jury that he was insane at the time of the killing and his counsel, Mr. Pashley [228] worked hard to lay a foundation for such

---

[225] The title he is given in the newspapers is police surveyor.
[226] In Glossop Road.
[227] The *Sheffield Independent,* December 4, 1841, offered its readers the following information about the parties: 'He is aged 30, Mary Nall, his wife, was aged 28. He is a machine fitter a short, rather stiff man, with a sullen passionate countenance rendered more repulsive by the loss of his left eye. His wife was about his own size of good features, which a few years ago were probably handsome, and, as appeared on the inquest, a remarkably well made and healthy woman. We understand that she and her mother have been accustomed to work in the file manufactory at Dun works
[228] **Robert Pashley**, b. York, September 4, 1803; educ. Trinity College Cambridge; BA 1829 (double first); MA 1832; Fellow 1830-53; barrister, Inner Temple, November 17, 1837; QC July 1851; Assistant Judge, Middlesex Sessions 1856 to death; died May 19, 1859.

a defence. From Lucy Nall he got out that, about a month before the killing, Nall had been knocked down by a crane whilst working for Booth & Co at the railway station. The blow had cut open his head and left him senseless. This was not, she said, the first time he had suffered a head injury. She had known him flighty and foolish in liquor and said that when provoked he was very passionate. She spoke of the deceased's association with the man Hibbert, a man of bad character, who did not work and who was due to be transported. From the surgeon called to prove the cause of death, counsel extracted the concession that a blow on the head would increase the tendency to insanity and, in excitement, might produce madness and that, if the insanity was slight, previous indications of it might escape notice.

In his closing speech to the jury, Mr Pashley argued that Nall's conduct, as proved by not only his family but his wife's, showed insanity and that the blow on the head was the cause of it. Nall had a tendency to insanity on provocation and there had been provocation. True it was only by words but the law acknowledged a blow as provocation and what blow could equal this provocation? They had evidence that the prisoner was rejoicing in his reunion with his wife, that he treated her with all the kindness of a lover and then, provoked and driven into an insane passion by her ingratitude, had committed this unfortunate act. Then there was the affection he showed for his dead wife, quietly remaining in the house at his sister's bidding and returning to the body and acting towards it in a manner only to be accounted for on the ground of madness. Also the number of wounds inflicted was suggestive of a man in an unconscious frenzy. Given the scanty material he had to work with, it was a most able address.

The summing up, however, was very much against the prisoner. The judge told the jury that there were no circumstances which could reduce the case to one of manslaughter. The threat of infidelity was no legal justification. The discovery by a husband of his wife in the act of adultery was an extenuating circumstance, but that was very different from the present case. However hard it might seem to press upon the prisoner, he must say that the peace of society required that, when persons went about their business like other persons, it was not safe to infer insanity from their almost unnatural atrocity or inconceivable want of motive. The circumstances of this man's vagabond life seemed not incompatible with his being in a sort of middle region between right-mindedness and insanity. But the question was whether the prisoner was able to distinguish between right and wrong. If so, he was responsible for his acts. If not, he was unfortunate but not criminal. He admitted the extraordinary conduct of the prisoner after the commission of the act and, although there might be some moral extenuation in the eye of Omniscience, it was not such as the law could fathom. He advised the jury to dismiss from their minds the previous threats. They seemed to be rather in favour of the prisoner, as militating against his understanding, rather than to give proof of malice. If the jury were of the opinion that the prisoner could not distinguish between right and wrong then they would find him not guilty of murder on the ground of insanity.

The jury retired and, after a deliberation of about half an hour, returned and pronounced the prisoner guilty but with a recommendation to mercy.

The judge placed the black cap on his head and, silence having been called, addressed Nall:

> 'Robert Nall you have been convicted of the crime of wilful murder; and though the counsel addressing the jury in your favour endeavoured to impress upon the jury the belief that you were not at the time you committed this act altogether a reasonable man, I found it my duty to tell the jury and I feel it my duty to tell you now that the state of mind you were in was not such as legally to extenuate your crime You were responsible for your acts and in the interests of society you must suffer for it. Whether or not there may be in a moral point of view circumstances to extenuate, if not to justify, your conduct is a matter beyond my power or province to determine and I should be acting in a manner not such as the country has a right to demand from me, if I did not tell you, in spite of the recommendation of the jury, that I see nothing whatever to justify me in holding out any prospect whatever that the sentence of the law will not be carried into effect And with these remarks, entreating you to employ in the most profitable manner the short space of time that remains to you I have now to pronounce upon you the sentence of the law which is that you are taken hence to the prison from whence you came and thence to a place of execution; that you there be hanged by the neck till your body be dead and that your body then be buried within the precincts of the prison in which you shall have been confined after your conviction and may the Almighty have mercy upon your soul.'

Nall who had displayed no emotion whilst being sentenced was then removed from the dock.

Whilst awaiting execution he shared the condemned cell with 60-year-old Jonathan Taylor, who had also been convicted of wife murder at that Assize. During the weeks after their condemnation, they were visited by a total of five clergymen. At first both were hardened and careless in their conduct but, as the day of execution drew close, they began to shows signs of repentance, particularly Nall who at first had been the more hardened. On the Friday before they were due to hang they attended the condemned service in the prison chapel. They spent the whole of the Friday night in religious meditation and prayer in the condemned cell. On the Saturday, at 5:30 am they were removed from the cell to a small room between the courts. At 7, they were attended by the chaplain. Nall did not deny the justice of his sentence but Taylor persisted in asserting his innocence to the last. At about 11, a crowd began to gather in front of the castle wall. At quarter to 12, the halberdmen and a few bailiffs, with their wands, came from the Castle and took up station in front of the scaffold. As soon as the hour of 12 had tolled by the Castle clock, the execution party made its appearance on the scaffold. Nall mounted it with a very firm step. Shortly after 12 the bolt was drawn and both prisoners were dead. After hanging for an hour, their bodies were cut down and buried within the precincts of the prison.

Present in the large crowd which witnessed the execution were some from Sheffield who had travelled to York during the night on foot.

During his last days, Nall wrote to his parents and family, sending them a pearl case and a lock of his hair. He told them that he was resigned to his fate. He expressed regret that he had not heeded their advice and kept away from his wife, saying that if he had he would have been a comfort to them in their old age instead of a disgrace to the family.

After his execution his parents received a letter from the chaplain telling them that he 'spent his last moments in a very Christian like manner and appeared to meet his unhappy fate under the supporting influence of a good hope through grace.' The letter concluded 'Would that you were all at this moment as happy as poor Robert.'

Alfred Waddington, 1853 [229]

In about 1850 Alfred Waddington, a 17-year-old grinder who lived in Sheffield Park,[230] started courting 16-year-old Sarah Slater. Sarah who worked at Butcher's edge tool factory in Eyre Lane, wiping and preparing tools for sale, was extremely good looking ('of considerable personal attractions' as *The Times* reporter put it). The couple had known each other since childhood. Soon she was pregnant by him and in November, 1850 gave birth to a baby girl. Before the child was born, Waddington asked Sarah to marry him. She received the proposal with little enthusiasm. He had a poor work record, kept bad company and had in the past stood trial for robbery. She said she would only have him if he was steady and got them a home. He was convinced that the real reason she had turned him down was that she had a lover; he had heard rumours that she was keeping company with a wealthy man, who had taken her to London to see the Great Exhibition. It was an accusation which she hotly denied.

When the baby was a month old, Sarah brought affiliation proceedings and Waddington was ordered to pay 2s a week for the child's support. Their relationship now went from bad to worse. He began regularly to threaten her, telling her that he would murder her, 'play Rush upon her,'[231] 'blow her brains out.' In May, 1852 she took out a summons against him for assault and he was ordered by the magistrates to find sureties to keep the peace.

He was also failing to pay regularly under the affiliation order and, on August 16, she issued a summons against him for non-payment. Two days later they met by chance in the street. 'Why have you sent a policeman after me?' he demanded. 'Go about your business and you will find out on the morrow,' she replied. 'But I'll lose my job,' he pleaded. 'That's nothing to do with me,' said Sarah, 'You should have thought of that before.' 'I'll give you a sovereign on Saturday,' he promised but then in the next breath

---

[229] Knipe, op. cit., pp. 224-26; *Sheffield Independent*, August 21 and December 24, 1852 and January 15, 1853; *The Times*, December 22, 1852.

[230] At Lord Street.

[231] A reference to the murderer Rush. Rush was convicted at Norwich Assizes in 1849 of the murder of two brothers. His victims were shot as they investigated a noise at their front door. Disguised in a wig, mask and long cloak, Rush escaped in the fog. He was executed on April 21, 1849. Such was the notoriety of the case that his effigy was exhibited at Madame Tussaud's for more than a century after his death.

said she would not get a penny. 'Then you will have to go to Wakefield,' she told him, walking off.[232]

The child was at this time living with and being cared for by Sarah's mother in Sylvester Street.[233] Sarah herself was in lodgings in Brown Street,[234] working during the day and in the evenings attending reading classes at the Mechanics' Institute[235] with her friend Sarah Dobson.

In the early evening of August 18 (the day of her acrimonious encounter with Waddington) she and Sarah Dobson, who had been sitting on the front door step of the house in Sylvester Street practising reading, were just about to leave for the Institute when ten year old Martha Barlow from across the road called to take the child for a walk. They left her to it and set off for their class.

Martha Barlow's walk took her near some brick kilns at the bottom of Sylvester Lane. As she was passing them Waddington suddenly appeared. 'I'm going to take the child for a ta-ta,' he told her. 'You can't,' said the young girl 'its her bed-time.' Waddington's answer was to grab the baby and to run off with it up Strawberry Hall Lane. Martha ran back to the grandmother's as fast as she could and told what had happened. The two of them then set off along Clough Lane looking for the child. By now it was getting dark.

At around 8 o'clock, Waddington put his head round the door of the room where Sarah was having her reading class and told her to come out, she was wanted. As soon as she got outside he asked 'Where hast thou left thy child? Who hast thou left it with?' 'With Martha Barlow' she replied. 'She has fallen off a wall and broken her neck' he told her. 'If thou wants to see her alive, thou must come with me directly.' 'Surely not,' she said. Waddington then took a knife out of his pocket and pointing to blood on its blade, said 'This is thy child's blood. I have murdered it' and showed her some more blood on the back of his hand. 'Surely to the Lord you have not hurt the child,' she

---

[232] I.e. to Wakefield house of Correction for non-payment.
[233] Sylvester Street adjoined Hereford Street at the bottom of South Street (the Moor).
[234] Adjoining Paternoster Row.
[235] The Mechanics Institute stood at the junction of Surrey Street and Tudor Street on a site now occupied by the Sheffield Central Library.

cried. 'I have,' he said. She then ran off down the street towards the Music Hall.[236] Waddington gave chase and caught up with her saying 'Come with me, I will take thee to the child.' She crossed over into Eyre Lane with Waddington hard on her heels. 'How could you hurt the child?' she asked. 'I declare to God I have not hurt the child,' he said falling on his knees. 'Will you follow your child?' 'I will go anywhere for my child,' she replied. 'I have placed it,' he told her, 'where nobody can get it but myself. Before I will let it be a slave under anybody I will murder it.' He then said he had left it at Catherine Wainwright's house. Sarah said 'If you have, she will take it home.' He then looked her full in the face and said 'Ay, but it is not there and, if you don't follow me, I will go and kill it.' She went with him as far as Jessop Street but then announced that she was going no further and was going to her mother's. 'Thou canst either save they child's life or kill it' was his chilling response.

Sarah, by now on the verge of hysteria, ran off towards Ellin's wheel in Sylvester Gardens. Waddington chased after her, grabbed her round the waist and tried to stab her in the side. She broke free and ran off along Sylvester Street. He caught her again and, grabbing hold of her by the dress, tried to cut her throat but she kept her head down and the slash of the knife caught only the back of her neck. She put her hand to her neck and screamed 'Murder!' He cut her again, this time on the hands. 'Murder! Murder!' she yelled. A young lad, called Henry Lee, now came running up and shouted to Waddington to leave her alone. When he saw the knife, he too began to shout 'Murder' and threw a penny at Waddington which hit him. The distraction enabled Sarah to escape and run into her mother's house, a mere twenty yards away. Later she and her mother would set off in the general direction of the Town Hall looking for the child.

Shortly after his attempt on Sarah's life, Waddington bumped into Sarah Dobson. 'Where's Sarah Slater?' she asked. 'I've murdered her. This is her blood,' he said pointing to his hand. Then pulling out a knife he slashed her face with it, causing a deep gash. The young lass turned and ran for her life.

At around 2 am Waddington walked up to a watchman named Harry Soar in the

---

[236] In Surrey Street.

Park shouting 'Watch!' He told Soar to take him into custody and held out his wrists for the handcuffs to be put on. The watchman said he had no cause to do so. 'I've cut my child's head off,' said Waddington, at which the watchman seized him and took him to the Town Hall. There he was seen by Jackson, the night constable, who asked for his name. On hearing that it was Waddington, Jackson, knowing that there was a warrant out for a person of that name, asked if he was there for arrears of bastardy. 'No,' was the reply 'I've done something worse that will take me to York and hang me. I have cut my child's head off its body.' He said he wanted the superintendent of police to go as soon as possible to Cutlers' Wood (near Heeley)[237] where he would find the body. He had used a shoemaker's knife and had thrown it into the Sheaf near Turner's wheel.

At around 4 am, the superintendent, accompanied by Inspector Rogers, went to the wood and, after a little searching, found the body of a female child. It was apparently entire but, when they tried to lift it, the head rolled away down the embankment. There was much blood about. The place where it was found was about a mile and a half from the Mechanics' Institute and half a mile from Sylvester Gardens.

Later that morning, Waddington was taken before Raynor, the chief officer of police, who told him that the charge against him was a very serious one and asked him if he wished to have professional advice or his father sent for. He said he wanted to see his father and wished it to be known how the woman Slater had treated him. She had, he said, gone to London with a gentleman to visit the Great Exhibition and, on her return, he had asked her 'Are thou going to be a rich man's whore?' to which she replied that she would rather be a rich man's mistress than a poor man's wife. He also complained that he had not been allowed to see the child as much as he wished. He added 'I was very much attached to her. I can't think what could possess me to murder the child. I wish it had been Sarah. Raynor told him that that amounted to a confession of guilt. 'It is well known I have done it and I wish to meet it fair,' said Waddington.

The following day he asked to see Raynor again. Would Raynor have to give evidence of what he had said the day before? Raynor told him that he did not intend to

---

[237] Cutler's Wood was situated on the east bank of the Sheaf approximately 1,000 yards north of Christ Church Heeley and 250 yards to the west of Bramall Lane.

give evidence before the coroner. Waddington then said that he would like to have his life spared as she had behaved so ill to him.

On Thursday at noon he was brought before the Mayor and another magistrate in the Town Hall. The charge was read out and Raynor applied for a remand. Waddington was asked if he wished to go before the coroner when the case was investigated by him and said he did. During the hearing he looked round at the spectators with great unconcern and smiled on recognising an acquaintance. When, however, Raynor used the word murder, his firmness for a moment left him and he covered his face with his hands, only to resume his appearance of unconcern shortly after.

The inquest was held at the Town Hall the next day before Thomas Badger, the coroner. S.W. Turner, a local solicitor retained by the prisoner's father, attended to watch the proceedings on his behalf. After the surgeon[238] had given evidence of his findings on post-mortem examination, the child's body, stripped of its clothes, was carried into court in a basket. Waddington immediately covered his face and turned away. Sarah was then brought in. As soon as she saw the tiny corpse, she screamed 'My child! My child!' and uttered several piercing shrieks. In answer to a question from the coroner she confirmed that the body was that of her child, adding, as she looked down upon it, her face contorted with agony, 'Oh! Is he not a villain?' She was then helped fainting from the room. Invited to give his explanation to the jury, Waddington said nothing. The jury were quickly back with a verdict of murder and the coroner at once wrote out the warrant committing him to York.

He took his trial at the Winter Gaol Delivery, 1853 before Mr Justice Talfourd. He was represented by William Overend, a Sheffield-born barrister soon to take silk.[239] At the trial, Overend attempted to set up a defence of insanity. He put to Sarah Slater the allegation that she had visited London with another man. She roundly denied it. She had never been with any other man and her visit to the Great Exhibition had been with

---

[238] Mr Robert Roper of 85, West Bar.

[239] **William Overend**, born 1809; son of the Sheffield surgeon, Hall Overend; educated at Mr Piper's Academy, Norton; he had at one time contemplated becoming an attorney and had been articled to Mr Sangster of Leeds. He was called to the Bar in 1837 and appointed QC in 1855; he chaired the Sheffield Inundation Commission, 1864-65, which assessed compensation in the aftermath of the Sheffield Flood and was Chief Commissioner to the Inquiry into the Sheffield Trade Union Outrages, 1867; he died December 4, 1884.

her uncle and aunt. Mr Roper, who had conducted the post-mortem examination, was asked by Overend to examine the accused's head and went into a nearby room to do so. On his return, he confirmed that he had found an old scar on the right side of the head over the parietal bone. The scar had never properly healed. He agreed that it was evidence of a serious injury and that such injuries could produce a deposit under the bone which could lead to brain irritation, although he had seen no evidence of that in the prisoner's case. He confirmed that there was a disease known as homicidal monomania which could be described as an intellectual aberration, in which a person is liable to be seized with a sudden destructive impulse under which he might destroy those to whom he had been most fondly attached, or any person who might happen at the time to be involved in the subject of their delusion. Re-examined by the counsel for the Crown, Mr Roper said that he had seen the prisoner for quarter of an hour on the day after his arrest and he had seemed then to be perfectly sane. The Crown had earlier elicited from Sarah Dobson and Soar, the watchman, that when they saw him on the fatal night he appeared sober and perfectly well aware of what he was doing. The prosecution having closed its case, Overend rose to address the jury.

He was not ashamed to confess, he said, that he rose to address them with considerable emotion and anxiety. He could not feel that the life of a fellow being was reposed in his hands without also feeling, at the same time, the great weight and responsibility that attached to him. Notwithstanding that he hoped to discharge his duty fairly to the prisoner. But perhaps there had been few advocates to whose lot it had fallen to confess as he did, appearing there for the prisoner, that his client had taken away the life of his child, his own offspring, that he had also attempted to commit murder on the girl of his heart and his affection; and also that he had attempted to murder another person against whom he could not possibly have any grudge, but with whom he had lived on terms of amity up to that moment. He had to admit all these facts. What then was the issue that was left for the jury to try? Not whether the prisoner had taken away life, but whether at the moment he did so he was a responsible agent - whether he was not acting under a sudden impulse like that which the medical man had said might occur when under a homicidal monomania? His learned friend had said that there was a presumption in law that a man was sane until the contrary was proved. But there was a presumption still stronger than that, namely that every man was innocent until proved to be guilty.

They would not require much further proof of insanity than the circumstances they had heard detailed in evidence. Lord Denman, in the case of Oxford tried for shooting at the Queen, defined the law as to insanity, that a person must be taken to be of sound mind till the contrary is shown, but a person might commit a criminal act and not be responsible. If some controlling disease was the acting power within him which he could not resist then he would not be responsible. But the question was whether the person so labouring under that species of insanity was quite aware of the nature character and consequences of the act committed or, in other words, whether he was under the influence of a diseased mind and was really unconscious of what he was doing at the time he committed the act. It might be contended that it was a dangerous doctrine to adduce the crime as evidence of insanity, but he believed that there were cases in which the crime itself could be brought forward as proof that a person was suffering under insanity. This young man, having been brought up from childhood with the young woman Slater, at the age of seventeen, formed an attachment with her which had continued up to the present time and the result of which intimacy was the birth of this child when its mother was not above seventeen. It was evidently the prisoner's first attachment and had continued up to this time, and the only reason that they had not married was that he was not, as she thought, in a position to support her. The facts showed that the prisoner having taken the child from the girl Barlow, intending to take it for a walk, was seized with a sudden impulse and cut off the child's head; and that then, whilst still labouring under the same diseased state of mind, he rushed back to the Mechanics' Institution, called out its mother and showing her his hands, covered with the child's blood, told her he had murdered it. Did they suppose that any man in his senses having committed a murder would immediately afterwards go into a room, where thirty or forty persons were assembled, call the mother out and then proclaim to her the deed that he had done and show his hands covered with blood and the knife with which he had severed its head from its body? If the prisoner, immediately after the murder of his child and the attempted murder of its mother, had committed suicide, would not the jury have said that he had done so whilst labouring under temporary insanity? He pointed out as proof of insanity, the prisoner's disregard of personal safety in going into a room in which thirty persons were; in calling the mother out; in acknowledging the murder to her in the public street when she might have made an outcry; his various and inconsistent statements to the mother; his saying one moment he had broken its neck, the next that he had murdered it and showing the bloody knife; the next moment falling down upon his knees in the street and calling God to witness that he had not hurt it; his declaring afterwards that it was where no-one could find it; then that it was at Mrs Wainwright's; his afterwards attempting to cut the mother's throat; his statement to Sarah Dobson that he had murdered Sarah Slater when in fact he had not done so, but had murdered the child whom he did not name; his onslaught upon Dobson and the attempt upon her life though she was a person against whom he could have no grudge. All these were consistent only with the prisoner's insanity. Everything was inconsistent with his sanity. The prisoner declared to Mr Raynor that he loved his child and that he did not know what possessed him to kill it. He had slain the thing he loved most. It was impossible to reconcile that with the prisoner's sanity.

The prisoner's statement to Mr Raynor showed that the feeling on his mind was that the young woman Slater wished to get rid of him; he spoke of her having been to London with another man; of her having said that she would rather be a rich man's mistress than a poor man's wife; all of which it turned out were untrue – were a perfect delusion and hallucination of his mind. There were indications in favour of the prisoner as showing the aberration of mind under which he then suffered. The mother of the child had told him that noon that she would have sent him to Wakefield. Supposing he had been drinking that afternoon and brooding over the circumstances, that would have produced the diseased action of the brain and impulse which caused him to destroy the object he loved best. He did not like to call the father or friends of the prisoner to speak to the injury he had received to the head, because he knew how their evidence would have been received, and therefore had desired the surgeon, an impartial man, to examine him. The surgeon had found the indentation of a severe wound of long standing and stated that it was not inconsistent with his having received a severe blow on the head that there should be a deposit of some matter which might act upon the brain and produce great excitement. It was said the prisoner was cool and collected when the surgeon saw him the next day. The very fact of his coolness proved insanity. Let them ask themselves if a man, having murdered his child, having attempted the murder of his lover and also that of her friend was possessed of his reason, would they not expect him to be flurried and agitated. But in this case there was the volcano, cool without and raging with fire within. They knew nothing of what became of the prisoner in the interval between nine o'clock at night and two in the morning but they might conceive that, when reason reasserted her power over his mind and when he became conscious of the acts he had done, they could imagine the remorse that attached to him, the misery and distress in which he would be placed and which led to his at once surrendering himself to the police. But up to that moment, when his disordered reason had begun to reassert its power, he still stood by the hallucination that had possessed his mind that the young woman had formed another attachment, that being in fact a delusion and one of the symptoms of his insanity. He left the case confident that they would do their duty to the country and the prisoner and that they would find that what this unfortunate young man had done he had not done criminally and ought not as a criminal to be responsible.

Mr Justice Talfourd then summed up. He stressed to the jury that 'it was most important for the security of human life that they should not hastily adopt the conclusion that the mere atrocity of an act must be taken as a reason why the person committing it must be insane. He was bound to tell them that, with whatever compassion they might regard the act, yet if the party knew when he did it that it would be the death of the child and that he was liable to punishment, then there would be no question but that the severe duty of finding the prisoner guilty of murder would be theirs. The question for them was: can you, as reasonable men looking at the evidence, as honest and reasonable men, say that in your opinion at the time the prisoner did the act he was afflicted, though it might be only temporarily, with a mental disease which prevented him from knowing and understanding the nature of the act which he committed? If you think that it was so, you will say not guilty on the ground of insanity. If, however, you think that looking at the facts you are bound to come to a contrary conclusion you will fearlessly do so.

The jury retired at ten minutes past one and were back at five to two with a verdict of guilty of murder. The crier called for silence whilst sentence of death was passed and the judge, having donned the black cap, addressed Waddington:

> Alfred Waddington, it is unnecessary for me to say a word with regard to the nature of the crime of which you are now to receive the last judgment of the law because I perceive that, almost as soon as the crime was committed, almost as soon as that guilty passion of revenge and jealousy which caused you to take the life of your innocent and unoffending child had subsided, which it did almost on the consummation of that crime, that you immediately awakened to a sense of the dreadful guilt which you had incurred and then sought to relieve yourself from unavailing anguish by making a confession of what you had done and giving yourself up into the hands of justice. I hope, therefore, that you are prepared to use for your everlasting advantage those few precious days which remain to you in this transitory life. I trust that you will so employ those days that you may obtain a portion in that pardon, which is held out to us through that great salvation which inestimable love has prepared for all those who seek it, which all of us need, and which may yet be extended even to you. As you will have during your few remaining days of your life the assistance of a minister of religion, who will with the greatest kindness endeavour to afford you consolations which your sad condition requires, and will wisely seek to promote your everlasting welfare, I can only now pray that the divine blessing may follow those endeavours. And to me nothing remains but to pass the sentence of the law, which is that you be taken hence to the place from whence you came and from thence to the place of execution and that you be hanged by the neck till you be dead and that your body be buried within the precincts of the prison and may God have mercy upon your soul.

Whilst passing sentence Mr Justice Talfourd displayed great emotion and sobbed audibly during its delivery. When he referred to the pardon held out by Christ to those who seek it, Waddington himself burst into tears. Sentence having been passed he was handcuffed and removed from court.

He was executed on Saturday, January 8, 1853. James Barbour, who had been convicted of murder at same assize, had been due to hang with him but was, on the eve of execution, granted a temporary reprieve.[240] During his time in prison, Waddington displayed penitence and spent his final hours praying. A crowd, estimated by a Sheffield newspaper reporter at 8,000, gathered to watch him hang. He stepped onto the scaffold with a firm step, his last words before he was turned off were 'Lord Jesus receive my soul.' After the drop he struggled for only a short time. His body was buried within the prison behind the window of the condemned cell. He was 20 years old.

---

[240] Waddington and Barbour had on the Sunday before attended the prison chapel to hear the condemned sermon preached by the Rev. Sutton, the prison chaplain, who had taken as his text *Ezekiel*, xviii, v. 30.

Sylvester Street today. It was here that Waddington abducted Sarah Slater's child.

What remains today of Cutler's Wood where the body of Sarah Slater's murdered child was found.

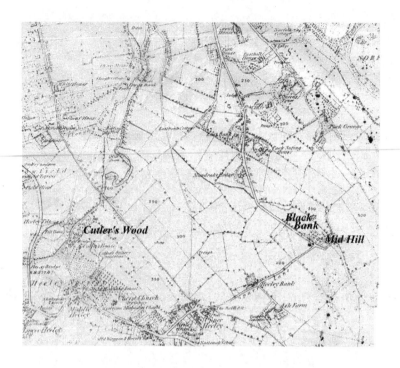

Ordnance Survey map of 1849 showing Cutler's Wood and Midhill,
the scenes of the Waddington and Barbour murders respectively.

The Royal Standard public house today. Barbour called in here shortly after murdering
Robinson at Midhill and it was here that the inquest upon his victim was opened.

James Barbour, 1853 [241]

At around 7 pm on Thursday September 3, 1852 two young boys who were picking blackberries in Appleyard's field at Midhill Black Bank,[242] found a body lying in the hedge bottom. They ran to fetch Mr Renton. He set off up the field. He took a servant with him and called to some Irish reapers who were working nearby to come and lend a hand. The body was that of a man and head and face were bloody. Renton went though the dead man's pockets. He had no money, no watch, nothing except a pair of lady's scissors and a couple of song-books, one with Robinson written on the cover. The police were sent for but by the time they arrived it was already getting dark. The body was placed on a cart and taken to the *Royal Standard* public house,[243] about a mile and a quarter away.

In the fading light a close search was made of the field. Five or six yards from where the body had lain the ground was bloody and much trodden, as if there had been a violent struggle, and a few yards beyond, stuffed into the hedge bottom, were a crushed silk hat and a heavily bloodstained silk handkerchief. Also found were an excise man's ink-bottle and a small stone bottle containing laudanum.[244]

Back at the public house, it was discovered that the dead man's clothes, like the song-book, were marked Robinson.

On the Friday a local surgeon, Mr Roper,[245] conducted a post mortem. He found that the body was that of a stout, well-made, muscular young man. There was a circular

---

[241] For press reports of the case see *The Times,* December 24, 1852 and January 1,10, 14 and 17, 1853 and *The Sheffield and Rotherham Independent*, September 11 and December 24, 1852 and January 1 and 15, 1853.

[242] *Sheffield and Rotherham Independent*, September 11, 1852 From the point where the river Sheaf crosses Suffolk road, the ground begins to rise rapidly towards East bank and Heeley bank. A little beyond Queen's Tower is Midhill, the residence of Mr W Renton. It is situated at a considerable elevation and commands a fine view of the town and surrounding country. Behind the house is a narrow valley, running down from the direction of Newfield Green between two steep hills. The public road terminates near Mr Renton's house. Beyond is a rude private road to fields which are occupied under the Duke of Norfolk by Mr Joseph Appleyard, farmer of Heeley bank. The fields on the east-side of the valley are in pasture. In one of them high on the hillside the body was found. On the west-side is a cornfield crossed by a footpath from Midhill to Newfield Green. This path commands a full view of the field called Black Bank and of the whole hedge side under which the body was found.

[243] In St Mary's Road.

[244] A preparation of opium in wine much used in Victorian times for pain relief.

[245] Robert Roper of 85, West Bar.

wound to the crown of the head, about two inches deep, and a similar wound behind the right ear. On the right jaw were four incised wounds, which ran down across the face, and a mark which looked like a powder burn. The jaw itself was fractured near the angle and the nose and the right orbit were also broken. When the skull was opened up, gun wadding, fragments of bone and several flattened pieces of no. 4 shot were found in the brain adjacent to the wound at the back of the head. There was more shot, this time unflattened, in the wound at the back of the ear. The stomach contained undigested duck meat and onion, which the surgeon thought had been eaten not more than three hours before death. He was in no doubt that the head wounds were the cause of death. They could not have been self-inflicted and, in his opinion, the deceased had probably been shot from behind near to the area of trampled and bloodied ground and his body then dragged over to the ditch and thrown in.

The police still had no idea who the dead man was. A local newspaper published a report claiming that the body was that of a local man called Scrimshaw, only for Scrimshaw to turn up alive and well.

On the Saturday a man named McDonald, who had read in the newspapers that the dead man had been dressed in the fashion of a Scotch packman[246] and that the name in his clothing was Robinson, asked to see the corpse. After doing so, he told the police that the body was that of Alexander Robinson, a Scotch packman in the employment of a Doncaster linen draper called Barbour. Barbour was sent for and confirmed the identification. He said that the deceased had worked for him for the last three and a half years as a salesman. He was 24 years of age, came from Dumfriesshire and was well able to take care of himself in a fair fight. He had left Doncaster on Monday, August 30, with a pack containing linen drapery goods and had on him a silver watch, key and guard which he, Barbour, had given him. He had been heading for Sheffield where it was intended that he should stay for four days, calling on customers, and then return to Doncaster on Thursday evening. He had not seen him since. He would have expected him over four days to sell £6 or £7 worth of goods.

Police inquiries established that the deceased had arrived in Sheffield on Monday

---

[246] Travelling salesman.

30th and taken lodgings at *Naylor's* public house in Watson's Walk. He had left those lodgings on Thursday September 2. While in Sheffield he had met with James Barbour, his employer's cousin. James had, until August, also worked for his cousin as a packman but had then been dismissed for embezzlement. He had then left for Scotland and had only been in Sheffield for a matter of days at the time of the murder. When he arrived he had with him a young man called McCormack, who was helping him collect monies owing for goods sold on his uncle's behalf, and the two of them had taken lodgings at the home of a man called Piggot.

At 1 pm on September 2, he and Robinson had lunched together at *Gray's* eating house in Watson's Walk in company with a licensee named Boot and two drapery assistants, McLelland and Fagin.[247] They had duck and potatoes with onion stuffing. Boot left as soon as he had finished his meal and, shortly afterwards the others adjourned to *Naylor's* [248] for a glass of porter. At this time Robinson was wearing his silver watch and guard and had with him a pack of drapery goods. As he was getting ready to leave, the landlord offered to change the silver he had collected on his rounds for gold. 'No,' said Robinson, 'I'm expecting to get some more this afternoon and I'll change it all later.' As the party left the public house, McLelland and Fagan asked Barbour where he was going. 'To introduce Robinson to some customers,' he told them. After that he intended to go to London because he believed the south was better for business. At the bottom of Watson's Walk the pair took their leave and, when they last saw Robinson and Barbour, they were walking together heading south. It was by now around 2 pm.

About an hour later George Hinde left his farm at Newfield Green and set off for Sheffield. It was a hot day and coming to a stile he sat down and took out his pipe. As he smoked, he saw two men coming from the direction of Sheffield. They looked like tea hawkers and he noticed that the taller man was carrying a bundle under his arm. As they got closer, he stood up saying 'I will give you room, gentlemen.' After they climbed over the stile the shorter of the two said 'What are you doing here? You should

---

[247] M'lelland and Fagan were drapery assistants employed by Mr Hyslop of West Street.
[248] The premises referred to are almost certainly Naylor's *Wine Vaults* at 20, Watson's Walk (see White's *Sheffield Directory*, 1852).

have some employment.' 'I have as much right sitting here smoking a whiff of tobacco as you have,' Hinde told him. The stile was less than 700 yards from the place where Robinson's corpse would be found that evening.

Christopher Corbett, coming from Newfield by a little used footpath, also saw the two men. They were travelling in the opposite direction to him and one was carrying a pack. They were about 300 yards beyond the stile when he passed them. Soon after this one of Mr Renton's lads, who was in the next field, heard two shots fired quickly, one after another. The sound came from Appleyard's field but a high hedge prevented him seeing who had fired them.

At about 4 pm Barbour entered the *Royal Standard.* He was alone, appeared hot and had a pack. He called for three pennyworth of gin and asked the landlord to look after the pack, saying he would collect it the following morning. The landlord locked it up in a closet and the next day handed it over to the police.

Having drunk his gin, Barbour said he wanted a cab. There was no cab-stand near and so a little boy was sent to fetch one from the stand at Moor Head, some 700 to 800 yards away. He also asked for a brush to brush his shoes and the bottom of his trousers, which were covered in mud and clay. Between the public house and the place where the body was found was a number of clay fields.

When the cab came Barbour told the driver to take him to the *Rein Deer* in Devonshire Street.[249] The cabman, surprised that he was wanted for so short a journey (it was only a mile or so away), would later remember his fare.

At the *Rein Deer*, Barbour met McCormack and bought him a drink. He also got the landlady, Mrs Swann, to change him £2 of silver for gold. Shortly after he went back to his lodgings and sent McCormack out for some gin. When he got back Piggot and a couple of his lodgers joined them for a drink. As they were chatting, Piggot asked what time it was, at which Barbour pulled a silver watch out of his trouser pocket. 'Hello', said Piggot 'have you got a watch, Mr Barbour? 'Yes,' replied Barbour, 'I sold it some time ago but, not having been paid for it, I took it back.' At about 11 o'clock he and McCormack retired to bed. On entering the bedroom he placed the watch on the

---

[249] 111, Devonshire Street.

dressing table. McCormack, who had never seen it before, asked him where he had got it. 'Oh,' said Barbour, ' I had it in pledge but I did not like to tell.' The following evening, he no longer had the watch. McCormack asked him where it was. 'It's met with an accident and is with a watchmaker' was the answer. If that was true, it was very speedily repaired, for, when he met McCormack in the *Rein Deer* at 2 pm on the Saturday, he took the watch out and asked McCormack to pawn it for him at *Beet's* pawn shop in West Street. He told him to pledge it for £2 and to give the name William Smith of Glossop Road. McCormack, after initially refusing, agreed to do what Barbour asked and, on his return, handed to him a pawn ticket and thirty shillings explaining that that was all the shop would give.

The inquest into Robinson's death opened at 5 pm on Saturday before Joseph Badger, the Deputy Coroner, and a jury of fifteen at the *Royal Standard*. The jury viewed the body and also went to look at the place where body had been found. The evidence of those who found it was taken and then the hearing was adjourned until the following Wednesday at the Town Hall.

In the course of the Saturday, Piggot had learned of the murder from his daughter and, when Barbour came in between 8 and 9 pm, he told him about it, adding 'I'm off to see the body.' 'Do,' said Barbour, 'and see if you can get to know who it is.' Piggot invited him to come with him but Barbour refused saying he didn't like to see such sights. It was around 11 pm when Piggot got back. On hearing him come in, Barbour sent McCormack downstairs to ask who the dead man was. He returned with the information that he had the name Robinson or Robertson on his linen.

The next morning Barbour questioned Piggot further.

> 'Did you actually see the body?'
>
> 'No.'
>
> 'Are you going again?'
>
> 'I've no money.'
>
> 'Go and get a glass at my expense,' said Barbour handing him a shilling.
>
> 'Come with me.'

'No, I knew him when he lived in Doncaster and for that reason I should not like to see him.'

On Piggot's return Barbour again plied him with questions:

'Who is it? Is anyone suspected? Is he much hurt?'
'He is dreadfully cut and shot and a bottle containing laudanum has been found nearby the body.'
'If some laudanum were found inside him, do you think that the jury would bring in that he had done away with himself?'
'No. He is so dreadfully cut and he would not have gone where he was found if he had wanted to do away with himself.'

After some further talk, Barbour proffered the opinion that there must be a woman involved somewhere.

The police by now knew that Robinson had been in the company of Barbour at *Naylor's* public house on the Thursday, and Raynor, the chief constable, decided to send for him. Barbour told him that the two of them had dined together on the Thursday and had parted near the New Market at Watson's Walk, Robinson's parting words being that he was going to Doncaster at 6 o'clock.

On his return, Barbour was full of himself. 'I have been to a larger house than yours,' he told Piggot. 'I have been to Raynor's house[250] giving evidence about the dead man. Poor fellow, we were the best of friends. We ate, drank and slept together.'
'Earlier,' said Piggot, 'you were telling us that you only knew him slightly.' Barbour appeared nonplussed and did not answer.

Raynor was not the only police officer with whom Barbour discussed the murder that Sunday. Earlier he had stopped to chat about it in the street with Constable Aston, to whom he confided that the dead man had been seen in a cab at 6.30 pm on the Thursday night at the *Rein Deer* and had had a Doncaster woman with him. The police

---

[250]   Raynor lived at 57, Gell Street (White's *Sheffield Directory*, 1852).

made inquiry of the landlady, Mrs Swann. She was adamant that Robinson had not been in her house on the Thursday.

Early on Monday afternoon Barbour called in at the *Rein Deer*. 'What a shocking thing about this young man,' said the landlady 'Have you see the body?' 'No, I would not see it for £50,' he replied. 'But you were his companion. It's very queer that you did not mention it on Saturday and that you did not go to the funeral.' Barbour ignored the comment! 'We dined together on Thursday,' he continued, 'and when we parted I shook hands with him and said 'I am going to Scotland and, if you have anything for your mother or sister, I shall be glad to have it,' and I have not seen him since.' He added that his uncle would lose £500 by the murder, as he had lost 3,000 customers in Sheffield.

After leaving the public house, Barbour bought some chloroform which he told the druggist he wanted for his wife's toothache. This was a lie: he had no wife.

Before the afternoon was out, Raynor, who had by now learned that the pack left by Barbour at the *Royal Standard* was Robinson's, had him arrested. By chance the cab driver, who drove him and the arresting officer to the Town Hall, was the one who had driven him from the *Royal Standard* to the *Rein Deer* on the fatal Thursday and he immediately recognised him. At the Town Hall Barbour was searched. He had on him £2.14.0 in money, a receipt for a registered postal letter, addressed to John Barbour, Bowness near Carlisle dated September 3, and a pawn ticket. He told Raynor he was unemployed and had received no money from McCormack. He said that the deceased had given him his pack to take care of when they parted. Asked about the pawn ticket, he replied 'Oh! I bought it off a man in West Street.' The police took the ticket to the pawn-shop and recovered the watch. They showed it to him. Had he ever seen it before? 'Eight months ago,' he replied. The answer was literally true: his uncle had in the past loaned him the watch but then taken it off him when he discovered that he had pawned it. Later that day it was shown to the uncle who identified it as the one he had given to Robinson. The landlord of the *Royal Standard* also attended the police office and identified Barbour as the man who had left the pack with him.

On the Tuesday Barbour and McCormack, who had also been arrested, were taken before the town's magistrates. The chairman asked them if they wished to go before the coroner and both said that they did.

The inquest resumed the next day with Barbour in attendance, represented by Mr Turner, a local solicitor. The *Sheffield Independent* noted that he was a stout built man, with a remarkably short neck, a strong muscular frame and heavy set features. When the hearing got under way Mr Renton, who was on the jury, was sworn as a witness and gave evidence of the finding of the body. At 1.30 the court adjourned until 3 pm. When it sat again one of the jury, a Pond Street druggist called Rawson, began to be difficult. Clearly the worse for drink, he was warned about his behaviour and when he took no notice discharged. At 7 pm the court adjourned, the deputy coroner announcing that it would sit again at 2:30 pm tomorrow.

On the Thursday, shortly before the court sat, the witness Corbett was asked to view a group of men in the prison yard and picked out Barbour who, he said, was like the smaller of the two men he had seen. However, when called to give evidence before the jury and asked if he could see in court either of the men he had passed in the field, he said he would not like to commit himself. Seeing the deceased's clothing had, he explained, caused him to doubt whether his earlier identification had been correct.

Hinde was also to be called that day. Before he gave evidence he was taken to a side room in which were Barbour and three other men. He picked out Barbour immediately, saying to him 'Did you not see me in my smock coat ont' stile?' 'Never!' replied Barbour. In the witness box he told the court that he was certain that Barbour was the man who had spoken to him that Thursday afternoon. Not only did he recognise his face but he recognised his voice.

Barbour, on being cautioned and asked if he had anything to say in answer to the evidence, read from a document given to him by his solicitor: 'I am not guilty of this supposed murder and if sent for trial I reserve my defence to the charge.'

The deputy coroner then summed up and, after a twenty-minute retirement, the jury came back with a verdict of wilful murder against Barbour. The coroner immediately made out a warrant for his commitment to York. McCormack, who had been admitted a witness at the inquest, was then called in and told that he would be remanded in custody until the magistrates had consulted as to the means to secure his attendance at the trial.

On Friday September 10, Barbour was taken to York by train. As he left, he maintained his composure and affected an air of indifference. However, at Masborough, he was seen weeping. He there spoke to a railway employee, to whom he owed money, telling him that he was confident he would be acquitted.

His trial began on Tuesday December 21, 1852, before Mr Justice Talfourd at the York Winter Gaol Delivery. Prosecuting counsel, William Overend, opening the case to the jury, told them that the dead man had been in the prisoner's company at lunchtime on Thursday September 3; that the two of them had been last seen together 600 yards from the murder spot and that at around this time the sound of shots had been heard; at 4 o'clock the prisoner arrived at the *Royal Standard* public house hot, dirty and in possession of Robinson's pack which had blood on it. On his return to Sheffield he was seen in possession of a silver watch which he never had before. The next day he got McCormack to pawn it in a false name. He had made contradictory statements and, for a man out of work, he had been very free with his money. Shortly before his arrest he had purchased a large quantity of chloroform with the intention, submitted the Crown, of using it to do away with himself.

The inquest witnesses were then called. When the landlord of the *Royal Standard* gave evidence defence counsel, Serjeant Wilkins,[251] put it to him that he had told a number of people, whose names he gave, that Robinson had been in his public house on the Thursday afternoon and had sung a scotch song to the assembled company. He denied ever having said such a thing and was adamant that Robinson had not been in his premises that day. The defence made strenuous efforts to discredit the evidence of Corbett and Hinde. With the former counsel made some headway, Corbett admitting that when he had first looked at the men in the prison yard he had not recognised any of them and that it was only when he was asked to look again that he had picked Barbour out; he also agreed that he had become more positive in his identification since talking

---

[251] In the nineteenth century there were three ranks or gradations of barrister, (King's) Queen's Counsel, Serjeant-at-Law and junior barrister. The order of serjeants-at-law, which in medieval times had enjoyed huge prestige, had been in decline since at least the eighteenth century. No further serjeants were created after 1868 and the order gradually dwindled away.

to Hinde. But with Hinde the serjeant got nowhere. He simply would not be budged. Barbour was the man who had spoken to him at the stile; he was sure of it.

Serjeant Wilkins called no defence witnesses and promptly launched into his closing speech. He warned the jury of the danger of convicting on circumstantial evidence and laid great stress on the fact that, if they brought in a mistaken verdict, there was no appeal and it could not be recalled. He suggested that, if one accepted the evidence of Hinde and Corbett as to the times at which they saw the two men crossing the fields, the prisoner could not have been one of them, for there would not have been time for him to get to the *Royal Standard* by 4 pm. The extensive nature of deceased's injuries pointed to more than one man being involved and if the prisoner had been one of them, he would have ended up covered in blood and yet he had no blood on him when he entered the *Royal Standard*. The small spots of blood on the pack proved nothing: they could easily have been caused by blood from a cut to a finger. The Crown had been quite unable to suggest any motive. Was it likely that the prisoner would have killed a man, whom he knew and was on good terms with, for the sake of £6 or £7 in money and a pack containing £10 worth of goods? The idea was ludicrous. The prisoner's possession of the pack and the watch was consistent with Robinson having given them to him to look after whilst he, Robinson, kept an assignation with a woman. His lies about the watch might be due to vanity or panic. There was no evidence where the prisoner went after 2 pm. Corbett said the taller man of the pair he saw had a light coloured coat on and yet the deceased was wearing a dark coat. He invited them to acquit.

Mr Justice Talfourd in his summing up warned the jury not to be alarmed about the possibility of a mistaken verdict. If they were convinced that guilt was proved, and brought in a verdict accordingly, they would be doing their duty and would have nothing to reproach themselves with. He suggested they ignore the purchase of the chloroform. Serjeant Wilkins' points about times assumed that the witnesses' timings were precise but all of them had given only approximate times. It was in prisoner's favour that he had stayed in Sheffield after the murder. The most telling evidence against him was his being in possession of the dead man's watch and pack after the murder.

The jury retired at 2:55 and were back a quarter of an hour later with a verdict of guilty.

The judge, having put on the black cap, addressed Barbour:

'You have been found guilty, to my satisfaction, of one of the foulest murders which the course of my experience embraces...You for some secret grudge which you entertained against a man who was retained in the service of your cousin when you were dismissed - either for that or for a desire to possess yourself of some paltry gain, plundered his person and property. You sought an occasion to do this when he had completed his duties at Sheffield. You then led him away to a secluded spot and there either alone or with some confederate - alone as far as the evidence goes - you fell upon him suddenly and unawares, deprived him of life, sending him, without a moment's time for repentance of his sins or reflection, in the midst of youth - in the midst of life - in the midst of thoughtlessness to appear before the judgment seat of God. The law is more humane to you than you were to your unhappy victim. It allows you some days for repentance and contrition, during which you may humble your heart before the throne of Almighty grace and seek to obtain a share in that precious redemption which has been wrought for all of us, and which we all need and which may be extended even to the worst of sinners, who in deep contrition, penitence and prayer seek it in the appointed way God has given. You will have excellent advice and assistance in that prison in which the few remaining days of your life must be spent and I commit you to that care. Nothing remains for me but to pass upon you the awful sentence of the law, which is that you be taken from hence to the place from whence you came and from thence to a place of execution, there to be hanged by the neck till you be dead and that your body be afterwards buried within the precincts of the prison in which you have been confined. And may God in His infinite mercy have mercy upon your guilty soul.'

Barbour, who had remained perfectly calm and collected throughout, remarked with great coolness 'Thank you, my lord, I am innocent.' He was then handcuffed and led away.

He quickly set to work to try and overturn his conviction. On December 23, the day following the trial, he dictated to the Prison Chaplain a '*Confession*' which purported to exculpate him of the crime and blame it on McCormack. Present when it was dictated was a Mr Dixon of Bury, a friend of his brother who had attended throughout the trial. It was in these terms:

'I now divulge the secret that M'Cormack swore me to keep. I last saw Robinson at two o'clock on Thursday, the day the murder is supposed to have been committed. I was going on my business and I met M'Cormack near 3 o'clock the same day on Suffolk Road. He gave me a parcel to take to the *Royal Standard Inn*, to be left until he would call for it tomorrow. I took it there and got two three-pennyworth of gin afterwards. I sent for a cab and went to the *Rein Deer Inn*. I found M'Cormack there, playing at bagatelle. A little after 5 o'clock he gave me a watch. I put it in my pocket. I asked him where he got it. He told me the girl Sarah had got it from Robinson and gave it to him. During the same evening some one asked me what time it was. I pulled the watch out of my pocket and, on looking at M'Cormack, he winked at me and shook his head. I then thought that all was not right and put the watch back in my pocket and said that I had sold the watch some time ago and had not got paid for it and took it back. M'Cormack then went out and when he came in again, he sat down a little while and then we went to bed. This all took place on the Thursday night. On Friday a girl of the name of Linley came into Piggot's, 105, New Meadow Street and said there was a man found dead in the fields near to Mr Renton's; and on Saturday morning I went to the *Beehive* public house to see the newspaper, in which I saw it was one of the name of Scrimshaw which had been found. I then went to the *Rein Deer Inn* and had some porter when M'Cormack came in. He sat down. I then said 'I'll have nothing to do with the watch' and gave it back to him. I gave it him back. He took it. We had some mutton chops together. In the afternoon about 3 o'clock he went out and returned about twenty minutes afterwards. He then said he had pledged the watch and pressed upon me to take the duplicate. I refused two or three times and, through his persuasion, I got it into my fob pocket and on Saturday night we slept together at 105, New Meadow Street. William Piggot went to the *Royal Standard* and did not return until after we had got upstairs. I had got undressed and got into bed. M'Cormack was about half-undressed and, on hearing some one come in, he went downstairs again and said it was either Robinson or Rollinson. He then got into bed. On the Sunday morning we went out together for a walk and, going up Glossop road, it was then he told me about shooting Robinson and swore me to keep the secret. I did so. I said I would keep it and on the evening of the same day when we had got to bed, he told me that he gave the money which he took from Robinson unto the girl Sarah with whom he had been cohabiting and that she had gone away and that he did not expect to see her again; and on the Monday morning he was dressing himself while I was in bed. He took a pistol out of his coat pocket and showed it to me. He said 'That was the pistol that cooked Robinson's goose.' Those were the very words he used. He said 'I have often watched for him but I have caught him at last'. He went downstairs got his breakfast and went out. As I was going up West Street he came up to me and said he was going to hide the pistol. He went and hid it behind the Botanical Gardens; he went down a little lane that leads to a field; he opened the gate and put the pistol inside the loose wall near to the wall of the Botanical Gardens. After M'Cormack had hid the pistol he said to me 'So help you God, you won't tell.' I did so. He gave me a cigar and we came together until we got to Glossop Road. On coming down Glossop Road M'Cormack told me he would not have the bother of Robinson going with his girl any more, as he was made safe and the girl was gone away. This is the statement M'Cormack made to me. I also further state that I saw M'Cormack with a white silk handkerchief with black spots on it on the Wednesday night which was the night before the murder.'

(Signed) JAMES BARBOUR

He also drew a plan showing where the pistol was hidden and a copy of this was forwarded to Raynor together with a brief summary of the confession. Raynor received the documents on the morning of Christmas day and went at once to the Botanical Gardens. So accurate was the plan that he found the pistol almost straightaway. It was of a common make and, although now rusty, appeared new; with it were two twists of paper one containing gunpowder, the other no. 4 shot.

A few days later Dixon travelled to Sheffield, saw Raynor and asked him to have McCormack arrested. Raynor went to consult with the town's magistrates. They decided to grant Dixon and Barbour's solicitor, Turner, an interview, present at which was Mr Branson, the prosecution solicitor. Dixon laid before them a copy of Barbour's confession. They were unimpressed, taking the view that it tended to confirm rather than disprove his guilt.

The press took the same line, pointing out that it was completely silent as to his movements between 2 and 4 pm on the day of the murder. In an attempt to deal with this criticism, Barbour made the following statement through the prison chaplain:

> 'After Robinson had left me I went down the Wicker, past the *Twelve O'clock*, to Burton Terrace. I called at many places about there and I think I called at Mrs Young's. I then went down Pond Street to the house of a customer whom I did not find at home. I then went down Suffolk Road and met M'Cormack.'

The newspapers, on receiving this tit-bit, were straight round to Mrs Young's. She said Barbour had visited, but on the Tuesday not the Thursday. This failure, by the only witness he had named to back up what he said, hardly inspired confidence.

Preparations went ahead for Barbour's execution, it being intended that he should be hanged along with Waddington on Saturday January 8th.

Dixon, however, did not give up. A memorial signed by a number of Bury's leading citizens was sent to the Home Secretary, Lord Palmerston, asking him to commute the death sentence. In it they referred to the confession, to the fact that Barbour had always protested his innocence and to his good character and claimed that he had an alibi for the time of the murder and had given an explanation of his possession of the articles of the deceased, which overturned much of the evidence called against him at his trial. Dixon also wrote a letter to *The Times* in which he stated that the circumstances in which Barbour's confession had been made left him in no doubt of its truth. Before embarking upon it he had been warned of the awful consequences of falsely accusing another and had replied 'I know my doom and am prepared to die and God knows I am innocent.' He went on to set out the results of inquiries which he himself had made at Sheffield. He had found a Mrs Rutter, who had confirmed she did owe Barbour money. Piggot, with whom Barbour lodged at the time of the murder, had been seen and given him a good character but had complained of McCormack keeping late hours. He had also found a Mrs Hewitt, who said that Robinson had called on her at quarter to half past three on the day he was murdered to collect some money she owed him; when he left she saw him go across the road to a man who was almost as tall as he, and the two of them then set off together; she was sure that this other man was not Barbour.

And the efforts bore fruit. Late on Friday a messenger from the Home Office arrived at York Castle, with a one-week reprieve. It was believed that Dixon had enlisted the help of Mr Lee, the MP for Bury and under-secretary of the colonies, and that his voice had proved influential.

Lest Barbour's hopes be raised unduly, a further message was despatched from the Home Office the next day, instructing the prison governor to make clear to him that 'his final chance of having his life spared depended upon the production of the newly promised testimony and that, as far as the evidence already produced went, there was no reason for interfering with the due course of law.'

On the Sunday, two Home Office officials called on the mayor of Sheffield and left with him a letter. It enclosed a copy of the confession, the memorial and Dixon's letter, and requested that he carry out an investigation.[252] The mayor immediately sent for the chief constable and asked him to have McCormack attend at the Town Hall. He came accompanied by Piggot, his landlord. On hearing the confession read out, he said at once that it was untrue and proceeded to give a detailed account of his movements on the day of the murder, naming persons who could confirm what he said. Raynor told the mayor that McCormack had given the same explanation when arrested back in September, that it had been investigated then and found to be fully borne out by other witnesses, so much so that he was discharged by the coroner. McCormack added that a short time before Barbour's trial, Mr Dixon and Mr Turner, the solicitor, had approached him in *Naylor's* public house, accused him of the crime and offered him money and a free passage to Australia if he would agree to leave the country. He had refused saying that to do so would bring suspicion on him, adding 'If I were guilty, I

---

[252] Barbour's was not the only nineteenth-century capital case in which the Home Office commissioned a post-conviction inquiry. In 1856 the Home Secretary, Sir George Cornewall Wallis, appointed 'the best known surgeon in London,' Sir Benjamin Collins Brodie to report upon the case of Dr William Smethurst, convicted at the Old Bailey of murder by poisoning and in 1882 the execution of Dr George Henry Lamson was postponed for three weeks to await evidence from America concerning his sanity: Jonathan Goodman (ed), *Medical Murders*, BCA London, 1992.

would go.' The mayor was so convinced by McCormack's explanation that he allowed him to leave the Town Hall upon his promising to return next day at 10 am.

On the Monday, the town magistrates began an inquiry. They told Barbour's solicitor, Mr Turner, that they would receive any evidence he wished to tender but he said he was not prepared with any, not having received any instructions from his client. The magistrates then proceeded to take a deposition from McCormack. In it, he said that at 1 pm on the day of the murder he went to the *Rein Deer* where he remained the rest of the afternoon, playing bagatelle with friends, whom he named, and was still doing so when Barbour came in at 5 o'clock. He had only ever met Robinson once and that was six months ago. He had never heard of him keeping company with any young woman. It was true that on the Sunday he went for a walk with Barbour along Glossop Road as far as Wilkinson Street, but then had left him to go to the half past ten service at the Queen Street chapel. He invited Barbour to come but he refused. On the Sunday afternoon, he went with Piggott to view the body and then the two of them went to look at the place where it had been found. On the Monday, the day Barbour claimed he had taken him to hide the pistol, he was doing his rounds all day, visiting customers. Between 8 and 11 am he called on upwards of twenty customers in Bridge Houses, the Wicker, then down Shalesmoor, Hoyle Street, Matthew Street and Shepherd Street. At 11 o'clock he called in at the *Black Horse* in Upper Allen Street, read the newspaper for an hour, and then went to Edward Street and Scotland Street calling on customers, and then on to an eating-house in Silver Street where he had some dinner. He left there just after 1 o'clock and set off on his round again, calling on customers in Snow Lane, Copper Street, Bower-spring, Spring Street, Workhouse Lane, Lambert Street, Pea-Croft, White-Croft, Pea-Croft again, Hollis-Croft, Garden Street, Broad Lane, Bailey Lane, Sim's-Croft, Townhead Street, Lee-Croft and West Bar Green. He went next to an eating-house for some tea and at half past five he went home. Soon after, Barbour came in.

Two penknife cutlers, Wharton and Cartwright, confirmed McCormack's account of his movements on the day of the murder. They particularly remembered the day since it was the day of the Cutlers' Feast and a holiday for them.

His movements on the Monday were confirmed by several of his customers and their receipt books. There was also evidence as to Barbour's movements that day. Charles Booth, a spring-knife cutler of Charles Street, said that at 9.30 am he was walking past the Botanical Gardens with Frederick Grayson and John Watson when, near to the walk which leads from the gardens to Ecclesall Road, they saw Barbour, who nodded to them. John Pearson, who lived at the *Ball in Tree* public house[253] near the Botanical Gardens, said that at about half past ten he had seen Barbour in Clarkehouse Road.

Martha Hewitt was the next to be called. She repeated to the magistrates what she had told Dixon about seeing the deceased at quarter past three on the day of the murder in the company of a man who was not Barbour.

Raynor told the magistrates that, whereas McCormack's account of his movements on the Thursday afternoon was detailed and corroborated by witnesses with whom he had had no chance to communicate, Barbour had spoken only in general terms as to his whereabouts, claiming he had been waiting on customers.

Piggott, with whom McCormack and Barbour lodged at the time of the murder, produced two letters which Barbour had written from York Castle prior to trial. In both he asked Piggott to give his 'best respects to Mr McCormack.'

At 8 pm the magistrates adjourned for the day. As far as the press were concerned, the evidence given had served not merely to exonerate McCormack but to confirm the correctness of the jury's verdict. The investigation concluded on the Wednesday and the magistrates' findings were immediately communicated to the Home Office. By now, all hope for Barbour was gone. On Thursday he was told the result of the inquiry and, later that day, the Prison Governor informed him that he had received a letter from the Home Secretary directing that the law must take its course. His execution would take place on Saturday. Still he continued to protest his innocence, refusing to attend the condemned service and threatening to disrupt it if compelled to go. When his cousin from Doncaster was shown in and asked what had become of Robinson's cash and cash-book, he was told 'You must find it out.' On the 5th he wrote a letter to his

---

[253] *Ball i' th' Tree* public house, Clarkehouse Road.

brother at Bowness, bidding him farewell and declaring his innocence. The press commented that, since his reprieve, he had appeared unmoved even when the body of Waddington, with whom he had so recently shared the condemned cell, was interred in the burial ground which could be seen from the cell window.

On Friday night he wrote a letter to a Doncaster clergyman asserting his innocence. At 10 pm he received a visit from the Governor, who urged him to confess and clear McCormack. 'I never said he did murder the man,' was his reply. After this, he spent some time relating to one of the warders some courting adventures of his youth. He was urged to pray and sing a hymn and consented to do so. At 1.30 am he retired to bed. At 5.30 the warders woke him. He told them he had had a very nice sleep and pleasant dreams. Between 8 and 10 am he engaged fervently in prayer and, at 10, asked for the chaplain, who was sent for from Fulford. Although by now plainly distressed, he still would not confess. At 11.15, he asked to see the chaplain again. He told him he was depressed for his parents and asked him to write to them, which the chaplain agreed to do. 'Then sir, I am guilty,' he declared. 'I alone committed the murder.' He asked to receive the sacrament again and, having done so, began to pray fervently. Soon after he was pinioned and now became extremely agitated and distressed. When led to the scaffold he was plainly terrified and the only words he was able to get out were 'Lord, have mercy upon me.' His agony was increased when the elderly hangman failed in his first attempt to draw the bolt. A lengthy delay followed during which the hangman tried repeatedly to do so, eventually succeeding with the help of a halbardier. After he had been turned off, Barbour was still at first but then dreadfully convulsed for about a minute.

During the execution the rain fell in sheets and, in front of the scaffold, all that could be seen was an immense roof of umbrellas beneath which the watching spectators were sheltering. The crowd was estimated by one reporter at 8,000 but the *Sheffield Independent* thought that the true figure was between 2,000 and 3,000.

CHAPTER FOUR

Hanged at Armley Gaol, Leeds

In 1864 Leeds, which had for some years been campaigning for its own Assize, was made Assize town for the West Riding. Henceforth all Assize cases from the riding would be tried there and all capitally convicted prisoners from the riding would be hanged at the Borough Prison at Armley. York would continue as the Assize town for the east and north ridings with its Drop used only for the execution of prisoners from those areas.

The first Leeds execution took place in September 1864, when Joseph Myers from Sheffield and James Sargisson of Rotherham were hanged. It was an event which created huge excitement there and led to bitter controversy.

Joseph Myers

Joseph Myers was fond of drink and over the years, when in drink, had given his long-suffering wife Nancy many a beating. As they grew older their children stepped in when they could to protect her but they were not always there. They were not there in 1861 when he wounded her in the throat. He ought to have been jailed for this assault committed shortly after the birth of his last child, but Nancy refused to prosecute. In Spring 1864, after yet another savage beating, Nancy left. At around the same time, following an altercation with his employer, Myers was ordered to find sureties to keep the peace and, being unable to do so, was jailed for six months. He was not in gaol long, however, for Nancy managed to find two people to stand surety for him. One might have thought that he would have felt some gratitude to her for her efforts but not a bit of it. Following his release from prison he seemed worse disposed towards her than ever, threatening, when in drink, that he was going to cut her throat.

On June 8, 1864, he called at the home of Ann Marshall, a widow, and asked to borrow her late husband's razors. Knowing of the threats he had been making, she refused.

At around 9 am on Friday June 10, Mary Hoole, who had lodgings in the same building as the Myers,[254] saw Nancy come downstairs. She was fully dressed but had only one boot on. A few minutes later Myers appeared carrying the other boot and threw it down at her feet. 'If thou wants the boot, thou can take it and ram it in thy throat' was Nancy's response. It seems that Myers had earlier been wanting to pawn the boots to get money for drink and that it had been her refusal to agree which had led to this exchange. Things then quietened down. Nancy busied herself dressing the children, while Myers occupied himself trying to remove a nail from one of his boots with a pair of scissors. Half an hour or so later Mary Hoole saw the Myers' young daughter enter the house carrying a jug of ale. She put it on the table and Myers quickly drank the beer off. Nancy, who had in the meantime been hanging out washing in the yard, now came back inside. Minutes later, Mary Hoole, working at the downstairs sink, heard a sound of scuffling. She turned round and saw Myers, on the stairs, pinning Nancy against a door with one hand and pointing a weapon at her throat with the other. Before she could say or do anything he had stabbed Nancy three or four times in the throat. She ran and pulled the badly injured woman away and, picking up the youngest Myers child, who was standing nearby watching, hurried both of them across the yard to Mrs Marshall's. As she was going out of the door, she looked back and saw Myers cutting his own throat: 'It was the same weapon which he had used to his wife' she would later explain '[and] it seemed very blunt for he had a great deal to do to cut his throat.' Nancy who was bleeding heavily from neck and chest was by now crying out: 'Oh! He has done me! He has done me at last!' Ten minutes later she was dead.

The police were quickly at the scene. PC Marshall found Myers lying on the floor of No 7. His throat was cut and he seemed to the officer to be in a very bad way. Myers called him over and said 'I've two or three words to say to you policeman.' 'I don't

---

[254] The Myers lived at House No. 7, court 5 (Hill's Square), Hoyle Street.

want to hear anything you've got to say' replied the officer, mindful of the law's then prohibition upon police interrogation of suspects. 'I've done it,' said Myers, 'and I hope the b.... is dead.' He then pointed to a knife which was lying on a nearby table and said 'Give me the knife and let me finish myself.' Instead of doing so, the officer bandaged the wound as best he could and took him off to the Infirmary. On the way to the hospital Myers asked him several times if his wife was dead and the officer replied each time that he thought not. Myers said he had stabbed her with a scissor blade. He repeated that he hoped she would die, adding 'All I feel sorry for is the children.' A post-mortem examination established that the deceased had four wounds, one to the face, another to the throat, a third beneath the collar-bone and a fourth which had pierced the aorta. This was the mortal injury. The scissor blade used in the killing was found later that day amongst some washing in the maiden pot. It had a broken tip.

Released from the hospital into police custody, Myers was taken before the coroner and, the inquest jury having returned a verdict of murder against him, sent for trial.

He was tried at Leeds Town Hall on Tuesday August 9, 1864. Being the town's first ever murder trial, the case attracted a huge amount of interest and, long before the doors opened, the steps and the streets outside were thronged with an eager crowd, of whom only a fraction obtained admittance to the public gallery. Reporters noted that the side galleries of the court were full of women spectators. At 9 o'clock Myers was brought into the dock. He seemed very weak although the wound in his neck appeared to have healed. Mr Justice Keating asked him whether he had any counsel to defend him and, upon being told that he did not, he asked Mr Middleton, one of the barristers in court, to undertake his defence. The trial then got under way. Vernon Blackburn, who led for the prosecution opened the case to the jury, observing that he was 'unable to suggest any circumstance which would reduce the case to one of manslaughter.' Mary Hoole, Mrs Marshall, PC Jackson and the surgeon who had conducted the post-mortem were all called to give evidence. In cross-examination, Mr Middleton sought to establish that Myers was in a passion when he attacked his wife. The Crown having closed its case, Mr Middleton (described in newspaper reports as 'labouring under considerable emotion') rose to address the jury. The prisoner, he argued, had been provoked to kill by the deceased's conduct towards him and therefore his crime was manslaughter not murder. It was poor stuff but then he had come into the case at literally the last minute and there was in truth no defence.

The judge in summing up told the jury that provocation, such as would naturally and ordinarily create in a person an ungovernable passion, would reduce murder to manslaughter and said that they must ask themselves whether there was 'any trace of any such provocation,' adding that he himself had been unable to discover anything in the evidence which would reduce the crime from murder to manslaughter. After such a direction conviction was inevitable and the jury brought in a verdict of guilty of murder without leaving the jury-box.[255]

The clerk of arraigns then rose and in a voice choked with emotion asked Myers if he had anything to say why he should not die according to law?' Myers indicated that he had. Barely able to speak, owing to the wound to his throat, his words were repeated by the gaoler who stood next to him:

> 'I was drunk the night before and I had had a quart of ale that morning I committed the deed or I should not have done it. My wife said she would throw the bond up and have me committed to prison. I didn't know what I was doing, or I should not have killed her.'

He shed a few tears but then listened composedly as the judge passed sentence:

> 'Joseph Myers, you have been convicted of the crime of wilful murder, aggravated in your case by the circumstance that the person murdered was your own wife – she whom you had sworn to love and cherish. You say that you did not know what you did. I am bound to say that I see nothing in the evidence that has been adduced that can give any reasonable probability of your being in that state. I don't desire at all to aggravate the horror of your present position but I would earnestly entreat you to think on that position, to prepare yourself to die and to look and to endeavour to find that mercy hereafter which you cannot hope for here. The duty remains to me to pronounce upon you the sentence of the law, and that sentence is, that you be taken from the place where you now are to the place whence you came and thence to a place of public execution and there you shall hang by the neck until you die, and that your body shall be buried within the precincts of the prison where you shall last be confined; and may the Lord have mercy on your soul.'

A general 'Amen' was heard throughout the court as Myers was removed. He walked away very quietly.

---

[255] They took just three minutes to reach their verdict.

Leeds Town Hall where Myers and Sargisson stood trial.

Armley Prison soon after its opening.

Armley Prison today: the Gate House.

The doorway, cut into the outer wall of Armley prison through which Myers and Sargisson were brought out to be hanged.

*The drop at the Women's prison used for private executions
at York prison in the last quarter of the nineteenth century.*

The drop at the Women's prison as it appears today.

The execution of Myers and Sargisson

After sentence, Myers was taken back to Armley gaol where he had been held since his committal. In the days following his trial he seemed determined to brave matters out, refusing to express contrition or to pray for forgiveness for what he had done. But, following a meeting with his son at which the latter, at the urging of the chaplain, told him that he forgave him, his resolve broke. Beseeched to seek God's forgiveness he needed no second telling. In his last days he wrote to his son, his sister and his cousin expressing his remorse for his crime. He also made gifts of scissors to the chaplain and to each of the latter's two daughters as an acknowledgement of the kindness he had received at his hands.[256]

The date fixed for the execution was Saturday, September 10. The work of building

---

[256] Not perhaps the most suitable or appropriate gift in the circumstances.

the scaffold commenced on the Friday. Constructed of rough timber and erected in front of one of the towers of the prison gate-house, it would be reached by the scaffold party via a doorway which had been cut into the outer wall. By 6 pm not only was the scaffold in place but so too were the barricades which had been erected to keep the crowd back. Armley prison, built in 1847, stood on the outskirts of the town. 'It has,' wrote the reporter of the *Sheffield Independent* 'the appearance of a baronial mansion situated amongst pleasant fields.' And it was in these fields that the spectators would gather the next morning.

Anticipating that the occasion would attract a huge crowd, no fewer than 200 police officers were despatched to the prison late on Friday afternoon where they would remain until after the execution.

Askern, the York hangman, had been engaged to act as executioner. There had been some talk of bringing Calcraft [257] up from London but Askern had, it seems, undercut him. He arrived on the Friday afternoon and went out onto the scaffold only to be driven off by hoots and shouts from the crowd.

On the Saturday, Myers and Sargisson, who was due to hang with him for the Roche Abbey murder, took a light breakfast at 7 and then spent their time praying with the prison chaplain. At 8.30 Askern arrived to pinion them and was apparently so overcome with emotion that he wept as he strapped their hands behind them. As they were being secured, Sargisson was heard to ask Myers 'Are you happy, lad?' 'Aye I am' came the reply. The prison surgeon clearly concerned about the wound to Myers throat now stepped in and put a plaster on it.

Meanwhile, outside the prison the crowd, which had begun to gather at first light, was growing. The majority of spectators came from Leeds itself but some were from outlying villages and a few from Sheffield. Farmers' carts, which had been used to bring people in, could be seen drawn up and the makeshift stands which local residents had erected (one above the toll house roof, another at the rear of a private house and a third in a field) were filling up. To enable them to get a clear view of proceedings,

---

[257] Calcraft was the Newgate hangman from 1829-74. He was notorious for the short drops he gave. Slow death from strangulation was almost a trademark of his executions and it was well known for him or his assistant to appear under the scaffold and hang on to the victim's legs to speed his death. He was in his 70s when he finally retired.

newspaper reporters were admitted to the garden immediately in front of the gatehouse. By 8.30 the crowd was enormous, estimated by one reporter at not less than 30,000 by another at between 80,000 and 100,000.[258] It included a large number of women but 'few people from the better classes of society.' There was much chaffing and jesting. Card-sharps and thimble riggers were plying their trade and clergymen preaching from makeshift pulpits, decked with banners urging spectators to 'Flee before the wrath to come' and warning that 'The wages of sin are death.' One would later complain of the 'revolting depravity of a large portion of the crowd.'

As the prison bell began to strike nine, the execution party appeared on the scaffold, first the under-sheriff, then the chaplain and, last, the two condemned men each flanked by two warders. A shout of 'Hats off' went up amongst the crowd, which then fell silent. Both men knelt to pray. As soon as they had finished their devotions they were hooded and the nooses placed around their necks. Both could be heard uttering prayers and again from Sargisson came the question 'Are thou happy lad?' eliciting the same answer as before. Askern then drew the bolt and both men dropped out of sight, their bodies shielded from the view of the crowd by a black cloth which had been draped over the section of the gallows which lay below the platform. Sargisson seemed to die very hard and continued to struggle for several minutes. But, according to the Sheffield newspapers, Myers fared even worse. Several days before the execution he had asked that the executioner to give him an extra yard of rope, pointing out that he was able to breathe through the wound in his throat. After the trap had fallen, it immediately became apparent that the wound had opened up and that there was a hole in his neck big enough to admit a large pocket-handkerchief, from which blood was pouring out, and that he was breathing through it. The rasping sounds of his breathing could, claimed the press report, be heard for some twenty minutes. All this was later denied by

---

[258] Cf The *Leeds Mercury* 'As the hour of execution approached the spectators continued to pour in large numbers until the wide open space in front of the gaol and every available spot around were occupied. The roof of every house and mill, walls and even the lamp-posts were thronged with those anxious to witness the execution and there could not have been less than 80,000 to 100,000 people present. There were also some hundreds of spectators on the Burley Road and near Woodhouse Moor, but they would be unable, except with glasses, to witness the execution.'

the prison governor and chaplain: Myers, they declared, had died almost instantaneously.

The whole incident left a very nasty taste. The *Sheffield Telegraph*, in its report of the execution, observed sourly that 'Leeds had long been ambitious of the honour of hanging [criminals],' adding that it was particularly appropriate that it should do so, for the town:

> 'is always in sombre colours. It wears a funeral hue and is in perpetual mourning. In this respect it has a clear advantage over Sheffield. The new Town Hall, which, a few years ago in the purity of its complexion looked like a jewel in an Ethiope's ear, is gradually darkening and in a few more years it will look like a Town Hall built of burnt cork.'

The advent of private executions

The execution of Myers and Sargisson was not only the first public hanging at Leeds it was also the last. In 1868 parliament passed the Capital Punishment Amendment Act which provided that henceforth executions should be carried out within prison walls and out of public view and, while there were several executions on the York Drop between 1865 and 1868, at Leeds there were none.

Between 1868 and 1965 when capital punishment for murder was abolished, sixteen Sheffield murderers were executed either at Armley or Wakefield prisons (between 1905 and 1915 Wakefield, which had never been used before and would never be used thereafter for executions, was the principal hanging town in Yorkshire). They included Charlie Peace and the Fowler brothers hanged in 1925 for a gang murder but the majority were, like Myers, wife killers.

York prison continued to be used for executions until the late 1890s. After the 1868 Act had come into force executions were at first carried out on a temporary scaffold in the prison yard but later from a balcony created by knocking out a cell wall in the old

Women's prison. The last York hanging occurred in 1896.[259] Three years later the prison was closed.

---

[259] Carlsen, a Swedish sailor, was executed there on December 22, 1896.

CHAPTER FIVE

Last Words

Of the 355[260] men and women executed at York between 1750 and 1864 just 28[261] were hanged for Sheffield crimes, an average of one every four years. This low rate of execution is not entirely surprising. In the era of 'the Bloody Code,' when capital punishment was at its height, the town had only a small, albeit fast growing, population (14,000 in 1736 rising to 65,000 by the end of the century) while in the period 1815 to 1864, when its population trebled, use of the death penalty plummeted.[262]

Of the 28 who died, all but one were men and at least seven were 21 or under. Just under half had killed. Of the rest one was executed for attempted murder, six for street robbery, three for burglary, two for child rape, one for arson, one for theft in a dwelling-house, one for forgery of bank notes, one for buggery and one for bestiality. Drink predictably was a factor in two out of three of the murders and robberies. Indeed, it all has a depressingly modern ring to it.

For cold-blooded killers like Fearne and Barbour few will feel pity, while the atrocious murders committed by Slack and Waddington produce feelings of horror and revulsion even 150 years on. For others, however, it is impossible not to feel sympathy. Lastley and Stevens, for example, hanged for a practical joke. They should never have been sent for trial let alone convicted and then the cruellest twist of all, the pardon which their townsfolk had won for them, arriving in York too late to save them. And what of young John Bennet, the only one caught and convicted out of all the Broom Hall rioters, put to death as an example to others, or 77 year old John Hoyland, whose life was falsely sworn away for the sake of the £40 statutory reward? That Spence

---

[260] The figure is taken from Knipe, op. cit.
[261] The figure of 28 does not include Moore who, although a Sheffielder, was executed for a crime committed in York.
[262] In 1815 there were some 200 capital crimes. In 1864 there were just four (treason, murder, piracy with violence and arson in the Queen's dockyards).

Broughton was a rogue, none, least of all he, would deny but he was not a killer and his exploits, like those of Turpin and Nevison, have a certain glamour about them.[263] And what of Mary Thorpe who, abandoned by her well heeled seducer, in desperation killed the child to which she had just given birth, having no means of supporting it and knowing that, if it came out that she had had a child, her prospects of getting respectable work or marrying would be negligible? Every assize produced its crop of wretched girls like Mary standing trial for their lives. Male juries were often merciful in such cases and, had she chosen to smother the child rather than strangle it, she might yet have escaped.

None of the 28 has any gravestone but we can still travel the route which the execution cart followed on its way to Tyburn, still visit the site of the Tyburn gallows tree and still see at the rear of the Crown Court building, the place (now covered by extensions to the court house) where the Drop stood between 1802 and 1868.

Hanging was a shameful and ignominious form of death. If it ever has been a painless mode of execution, it was not so then. Given only a short drop, culprits would usually die by slow strangulation, an agonising process during which their bodies would be horribly convulsed.[264] In 1709, an ex-soldier, John Smith, was hanged at the London Tyburn for burglary. Five minutes after he had been turned off a reprieve arrived and he was cut down. He was still alive and quickly recovered. Asked about his sensations, he replied that:

> 'at first he felt great pain, but that it gradually subsided, and the last thing he could remember was the appearance of a light in his eyes, after which he became quite insensible. But the greatest pain was, when he felt the blood returning to its proper channels.'[265]

---

[263] An account of Nevison's exploits is given in Appendix 1.

[264] Cf The description in the next day's *Times* of the hanging of John Tawell at Aylesbury on March 28, 1845:

> 'The length of drop allowed him was so little that he struggled most violently. His whole frame was convulsed: he writhed horribly, and his limbs rose and fell again repeatedly, while he wrung his hands, his arms having previously been pinioned, and continued to wring his hands for several minutes, they still being clasped, as though he had not left off praying. It was nearly ten minutes after the rope had been fixed before the contortions which indicated extreme suffering ceased.'

[265] The incident earned him the nick-name Half-Hanged Smith.

The 28 we have been concerned with appear to have died bravely, although some[266] were plainly terrified. What sustained them was the belief that they were about to exchange this world for a better one. Within a short time of a prisoner receiving the death sentence, the prison chaplain and other clergy would go to work, sparing no effort to try and bring him to a state of repentance and save his soul. Generally they were successful and most convicts who stepped onto the scaffold did so, firmly believing that God would forgive them their sins and grant them eternal life. In today's irreligious age such faith may seem naive but in Victoria's day men did not doubt 'the existence of an after life of rewards and punishments.' As Ensor memorably put it 'hell and heaven seemed as certain ... as tomorrow's sunrise and the Last Judgement as real as the week's balance sheet.'[267] If any question this, let them reflect on the last words exchanged between Sargisson and Myers on the scaffold at Armley:

'Are you happy, lad?'

'Aye, I am.'

---

266 E.g. Barbour.
267 Sir Robert Ensor, *England, 1870-1914*, Oxford History of England, 1936, p. 138.

Appendix 1

Pre 1750 executions [268]

Of those executed at York prior to 1750 at least four: Charles de Pascal, Robert Thomas Swedier, Thomas Empson and Charles Beaumond were natives of Sheffield. Beaumond was hung drawn and quartered, the other three hanged. All died for crimes of dishonesty committed away from Sheffield. De Pascal, executed in July 1579, had burgled a warehouse in Stonegate, York. Swedier, hanged in 1598, had broken into a house at Knaresborough. Empson went to the gallows in1646 for a highway robbery in Huddersfield. Beaumond's crime was coining, punishable at that date as high treason, hence the aggravated form of death penalty.[269] Swedier's body was, after execution, hanged in chains at Knaresborough forest. De Pascal was hanged at St. Leonard's Green Dykes, the three others died at Tyburn.

It is claimed that William Nevison, a highwayman hanged at Tyburn in 1684 had links with Sheffield. Born at Pontefract, he served for a time as a mercenary in the Spanish army but then returned to England soon after the Restoration and made robbery his profession. Harrison Ainsworth's description, in his novel, *Rookwood*, of Turpin's ride from London to York on Black Bess is based upon one of Nevison's exploits. In 1676

> 'having committed a robbery in London about sunrise and, finding he was known, [Nevison] fled to York, which place he reached by sunset the same evening on one mare. On his trial, he proved himself to have been at the Bowling Green at York on the evening the robbery was committed. A number of witnesses swore positively to him and he was acquitted.'[270]

For this feat Charles II gave him the nickname 'Swift Nick.' The same year he was tried and convicted at York Assizes of robbery and horse stealing. On his promising to reveal his accomplices he was reprieved, but then went back on his word and was conscripted into a regiment bound for Tangiers. However, he managed to escape and returned to highway robbery. Basing himself at Newark and York he plied his trade in Lincoln, Nottingham and Derby. In Spring 1684 he was arrested in a public house at Thorp near Wakefield and taken to York where he was hanged on March 15. It is claimed that he was in the habit of visiting a house at Gleadless and that a room in it was named after him. The story has been doubted since Gleadless lay well away from the Great North Road which was the scene of his operations.

---

[268] See Knipe, op.cit., pp. 9, 13, 14 and 25, Charles Drury, *A Sheaf of Essays by a Sheffield Antiquarian*, p 121.
[269] He was executed on July 28, 1602.
[270] Drury, op. cit, p. 21.

Appendix 2

Sheffield 1700 - 1864.

The earliest map of Sheffield is Gosling's Map of 1736. This shows a small town measuring half a mile from east to west and three-quarters of a mile from north to south, with hardly a building on the north side of the Don except at Bridge Houses. West Bar marked its north-west boundary and Coalpit Lane (now Cambridge street) its southern limit. It had 2,152 houses and just over thirty streets and lanes,[271] most of them extremely narrow.[272] Its principal public buildings were the parish Church (now the cathedral), the adjoining town hall, the Cutlers' Hall and the New Church, or St Paul's as it later came to be known. The population of the town at this date was just under 10,000 with a further 4,000 persons living in the outlying hamlets and townships which together with the town comprised the ecclesiastical parish of Sheffield.[273] Linked by road with Penistone to the east, Rotherham and Barnsley to the north and Chesterfield to the south, it had since 1710 had a stage wagon service for the carriage of goods to London.

By the time of the 1849 ordnance survey map Sheffield was a major industrial town famous for steel-making as well as cutlery. Its population now stood at 135,000 [274] with the built up area extending to Brook Hill on the west, Park Hill in the east and Moorfoot in the south and with steel works flanking the Don as far as Attercliffe. Over the past hundred years its communications with the outside world had been steadily

---

[271] The *Sheffield Register*, July 1732 lists them: High Street, Fargate, Balm Green, Hollin (or Blind) Lane, Red Croft, Townhead Street, Pinfold Lane, Church Lane, Ratten Row, Broad Lane, Westbar, Westbar Green, Scargill Croft, Figtree Lane (or New Street), Campo Lane, Hartshead, Snig Hill, Irish Cross, New Hall Street, Mill Sands, the Underwater, The Isle, Water Lane, Castle Green, Castle Green Head, Castle Fold, Castle Hill, Waingate, Bull Stake, Dixon Lane, Shude Hill, The Ponds, Jehu Lane, Pudding Lane (or King Street) and Truelove's Gutter.

[272] Cf Mary Walton, op. cit., p 108: 'Central streets were extraordinarily narrow. In parts of Red Lane, now Trippet Lane, which was quite a thoroughfare two carts could not pass one another. Church Lane with:

> Roofs nearly meeting a dark dreary street
> might justly be styled the robber's retreat.

whilst the side lanes and the Crofts were mere gennels.'

[273] The parish extended from Blackburn Brook to Stanage Pole and from Meers Brook to the Rivelin and a rather artificial boundary including Scraith Wood, part of Bagley Dike and the northern limit of Wincobank Wood (Mary Walton op. cit., p 25). It comprised six towsnships: Sheffield, Upper Hallam, Nether Hallam, Brightside Bierlow, Attercliffe and Ecclesall Bierlow.

[274] Population figures for the town for the period 1736-1861 are:

1736	14,105
1801	45,755
1821	65,275
1841	110,891
1851	135,307
1861	185,157

Pawson & Brailsford, op. cit., p 27

improving. In 1760 a stagecoach service to London was introduced and in 1819 the Sheffield canal was opened. 1838 saw the coming of the railway with a line opened between Sheffield and Rotherham. Two years later the line was extended to Derby thus creating a rail link to London. In 1807 a new Town Hall and court-house was built in Waingate. In 1835 the town was created a borough with power to manage its own affairs. Sketchley, in his *Sheffield Guide* of 1774, had commented on the black appearance of buildings in the town:

> '[They] ... in general are of Brick but from the great Quantity of Smoak occasioned by the Manufactory the recent erections are apt soon to be discoloured.'

However, some of the buildings now being erected, such as the Tontine (1785),[275] the General Infirmary (1795) and the new Cutlers' Hall (1832-33) at least possessed architectural merit. Areas such as Heeley were, in 1850, still rural and the General Cemetery, in what is now Cemetery Road, stood in open country, affording, as its designers intended, panoramic views of the town.

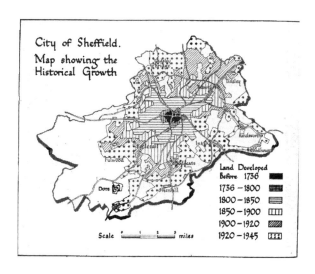

Map of the growth of Sheffield.

---

[275] The *Tontine* stood in Dixon Lane. Its history is given in Hunter's Hallamshire: 'On 29 September 1785 it was resolved at a meeting held in Sheffield to erect a commodious inn on a site 'where the Castle Barn now stands' at a cost of not less than £4,000, this sum to be raised by a Tontine. Each subscriber nominated a life during the continuance of which he was to receive an equal share of the rents and profits.' It was demolished in 1850 and the site used for the construction of the Norfolk Market.

Appendix 3

James Montgomery

James Montgomery was born in 1771 at Irvine in Scotland, the son of a Moravian minister. He was educated at Fulneck School near Leeds where he proved an able pupil. On leaving school he worked in shops at Mirfield and Wath before running away to London in the hope of selling the poems which he had been writing in his spare time. Having failed to find a publisher, he returned to Yorkshire where an advertisement for a literary assistant to the proprietor of the *Sheffield Register* caught his eye. He wrote for the job and got it. In 1794 his employer, Gales, fearing that he was about to be arrested for sedition, fled to America leaving Montgomery in charge of the newspaper.

In order to ensure that he did not himself fall foul of the authorities Montgomery changed the name of the paper to the *Iris* and protested in its editorials the journal's loyalty to the Crown. But all in vain. Shortly after Gales' flight he had printed and sold copies of a ballad, which he had found in the newspaper offices already set in type. The song which was about the Bastille and was mildly revolutionary in tone was declared seditious and, when it was discovered that Montgomery was the printer, he was immediately indicted. He was tried at West Riding Quarter Sessions in January 1795.

The jury was unwilling to convict but reluctantly did so after the presiding magistrates had refused to accept their first verdict. Montgomery was fined £20 and ordered to be imprisoned in York Castle for three months. On his release he returned to the helm of the *Iris*. He was soon in trouble again. In August 1795 soldiers, under the command of Colonel Athorpe, fired on a crowd of rioters. Two men were killed and others wounded. The account of the affair published in the Iris contained the following:

> 'A person, who shall be nameless, plunged with his horse among the unarmed, defenceless people and wounded with his sword men, women and children promiscuously.'

It was well known that the 'nameless person' was Athorpe and that what Montgomery had written was true, but Athorpe was a Sheffield magistrate and, confident that his fellow magistrates would support him, he prosecuted Montgomery for criminal libel. His confidence proved justified. Tried at the West Riding Quarter Sessions in January 1796 before a bench, which included Vicar Wilkinson, Montgomery was convicted, fined £30, ordered to be imprisoned in York Castle for six months and to find sureties for his future good behaviour.

After release from this sentence, his fortunes took a decided turn for the better. The *Iris* was proving a commercial success as was his poetry. Over the succeeding years his reputation in the town grew steadily, not least as a writer of hymns. In 1833 he was awarded a government pension of £200 a year. When he died in 1854 a statue was erected in his honour, which stands today in the grounds of Sheffield Cathedral.

Of particular interest for present purposes is the poetry, which he wrote during his confinement at York. Published in 1797 by Johnson of London in a volume entitled *'Prison Amusements and other Trifles Principally written during Nine Months of Confinement in the Castle of York'*, many of the poems were, according to the preface 'composed in bitter moments amid the horrors of a gaol under the pressure of sickness.' Extracts appear below:

a. The prison [276]

Now lets ramble o'er the green

And here let us the scene review
That's the old castle, this the new
Yonder the felons walk and there
the lady prisoners take the air
Behind are solitary cells
where hermits live like snails in shells   *Epistle I*

b. Prison routine

Each morning then; at five o'clock
The adamantine doors unlock;
Bolts bars and portals crash and thunder
The gates of iron burst asunder

When dressed I to the yard repair
And breakfast on the pure fresh air
But though this choice Castalian cheer
Keeps both the head and stomach clear

[For weighty reasons I make free
to mend the meal with toast and tea]
Breakfast dispatched I sometimes read
where periods without period crawl

---

[276] See also this verse carved on one of the walls of the felons' yard in 1820 and still visible today:

This prison is a place of care
A grave for men alive
A touchstone for to try a friend
No place for man to thrive

The author, 28-year-old Thomas Smith, was hanged at the New Drop on Saturday May 15, 1820 for sheep-stealing.

At half past ten or thereabouts,
My eyes are all upon the scout
To see the lounging post boy come
with letters or with news from home

Thus flow my morning hours along
The clock strikes one - I can't delay
For dinner comes but once a day   *Epistle I*

But lo the evening shadows fall
Broader and browner upon the wall
A warning voice like curfew bell
Commands each captive to his cell

My faithful dog and I retire
To play and chatter by the fire
Soon comes a turnkey with 'Good night sir'
And bolts the door with all his might, sir
Then to bed I repair   *Epistle II*

c. Keeping body and soul together

Not even in gaol can folk forget
To eat to drink and run in debt

Here each may as his means afford
dine like a pauper or a lord
And he who can't the cost defray
Is welcome, sir to fast and pray   *Epistle II*

d. Time weighs heavily on the prisoner

The days are only twelve hours long
Though captives often reckon here
Each day a month, each month a year   *Epistle I*

e. Cruel pleasures

This Robin with the blushing breast who
is ravished from his little nest
by barbarous boys who bind his leg
to make him flutter round a peg
See the glad captive spreads his wings
Mounts in a moment, mounts and sings
when suddenly the cruel chain
Twitches him back to prison again   *Epistle I*

f. The arrival of the judge at the court-house

Hark shrill and sonorous sounds
The trumpets dread summons I hear
Death's voice in the blood-chilling sound
Assaults the pale murderer's ear
What horror must stiffen his veins
At the pomp and the thunder of law
Guilt shudders and clings to his chains
Even innocence trembles with awe! [277]   *To Celia*

g. In the court-room

Across the green, behold the court
where jargon reigns and wigs resort
where bloody tongues fight bloodless battles
For life and death for straws and rattles
Where jurors yawn their patience out
And judges dream in spite of gout

---

[277] In a note at p.11 of the book Montgomery writes 'Every morning during the Assizes trumpets proclaim the entrance of the judge. These lines were written ... just at the time when Sentence of Death had been pronounced upon a murderer and his Wife, in violent fits, was carried by near the window of the writer.'

There on the outside of the door
(as sang a wicked wag of yore)
stands Mother Justice tall and thin
who never ventured in.[278]   *Epistle II*

h. Lawyers

With gown so black and wig so white
Symbolical of wrong and right
(For every lawyer lets his tongue
to any tenant right or wrong)
I'll split my wind pipe o'er a brief
and bawl for justice and for beef   *The Grumbler's*
Bow smile and simper to a client.   *petition*

James Montgomery.

---

[278] The reference is to the statue of Justice which stands atop the pediment at the entrance to the court-house.

Appendix 4

Spence Broughton's Last Letter to his Wife

York Castle,
April 14th, 1792

My Dear Eliza,

This is the last affectionate token thou wilt ever receive from my hand - an hand that trembles at my approaching dissolution, so soon, so very soon to ensue.

Before thou wilt open this last epistle of thine unfortunate husband, these eyes which overflow with tears of contrition, shall have ceased to weep, and this heart, now fluttering on the verge of eternity, shall beat no more.

I have prepared my mind to meet death without horror: and oh! how happy, had that death been the common visitation of nature. Be not discomforted, God will be your friend. In the solitude of my cell I have sought him. His spirit hath supported me - hath assisted me in my prayers, and many a time, in the moment of remorseful anguish, hath whispered peace: for my dear Eliza, I never added cruelty to injustice. Yet, tho' I have resolved to meet death without fear, one part of my awful sentence - a sentence aggravated by being merited, chills me with horror. When I reflect that my poor remains, the tokens of mortality must not sleep in peace, but be buffeted by the storms or heaven or parched by the summer's sun, while the traveller shrinks from them with disgust and terror, this consideration freezes my blood. This cell - this awful gloom - these irons, yea death itself is not so grievous. Why will the laws continue to sport with the wretched after life is at an end?

My Eliza, my friend, my wife, the last sad scene approaches, when I shall be no more. When I shall leave the world, and thee, my dear to its mercy - not only thee, but my unprotected children, the pledges of a love, through misfortune, through dissipation, through vice and infamy, on thy part unchanged. Ah, fool that I was, to think friendship could exist but with virtue. Had I listened to the advice thou has so often given me, we had been a happy family, respectable and respected. But it is past. That advice hath been slighted. I am doomed to an ignominious death, and thou and my children, horrid thought, to infamy. To thee alone I trust the education of those ill-fated creatures, whom I now more than ever love and weep for. Warn them to avoid GAMING of every description; that baneful vice which has caused their father to be suspended a long and lasting spectacle to feed the eye of curiosity. Teach them the ways of RELIGION in their early years, cause them to learn some trade, that business may fill their minds and leave no room for dissipation. When seated round your winter's fire, when the little innocents enquire after their unfortunate father, ah! tell them Gaming was his ruin - he neglected all religious duties - he never conversed with his heart in solitude; he stilled the upbraidings of conscience in the company of the lewd and profligate, and is hung on high a sad and dismal warning to after times. I see thee thus employed, while the tears trickle down that dear face, which I have so ill deserved.

Adieu, my Eliza! Adieu for ever! The morning appears for the last time to these sad eyes. Pleasant would death be to me on a sick bed, after my soul had made her peace with God. With God I hope her peace is made ... He is not a God all terror, but a God of mercy: on that mercy I rely and on the interposition of a Saviour. May my tears, my penitence and deep contrition, be acceptable to that Almighty Being, before whom I am shortly to appear.

Once more, Eliza, adieu for ever. The pen falls from my hand and slumbers overtake me. The next sleep will be the sleep of death.

Spence Broughton

Appendix 5

Gibbeting

The Murder Act, 1751 required judges to direct that the bodies of convicted murderers be either gibbeted or given for dissection. The power to order gibbeting was not, however, limited to cases of murder and could be imposed in cases of robbery and other capital felony, as Broughton's case demonstrates. [279]

In 1815, a little under twenty-five years after Broughton was gibbeted, a 21-year-old Derbyshire youth, Anthony Lingard, suffered the same fate.

On the morning of January 1, 1815 a local barmaid found 48-year-old Hannah Oliver, the keeper of a toll station on the Bakewell to Stoney Middleton road, lying dead in her toll-house. She had been strangled. The parish constable was sent for and set about interviewing the residents of nearby properties but without result. The only clue he had to go on was that the murderer had stolen the dead woman's shoes.

Shortly after the murder, Lingard called on a young woman, who was pregnant by him, and gave her the shoes and some money as an inducement to name some other man as the father. Shortly after, having heard talk that a pair of shoes had been stolen from the murdered woman, she returned them. Lingard tried to persuade her to keep them, saying that she had nothing to be afraid of for he had exchanged them for a pair of stockings, but she would not.

News of the gift reached the constable. He at once went to the young man's home and in a bedroom drawer found a pair of women's shoes. He showed them to a shoemaker in Stoney Middleton called Marsden who at once recognised them as ones he had made for the dead woman. He told the constable that when he made them he had inserted a motto 'Commit no crime' under the sole; he stripped them down and there, sure enough, was the motto. Lingard was arrested and taken before a magistrate to whom he confessed his guilt. He was committed to Derby Assizes and took his trial on Saturday March 11, 1815.[280] His confession was read to the jury. In it he said that he had visited Hannah on the night before her body was found, had lost his temper when she refused to give him money and strangled her. After offering the shoes to his girl friend he had hidden them in a haystack, but after a week or so, had retrieved them and put them in the drawer where the constable had found them. Convicted by the jury he was sentenced to death and it was ordered that his body be gibbeted close by the toll-house at Wardlow Mires.

It proved an expensive business for the county, the cost of the gibbeting coming to a little under £100.[281] The gibbet was demolished in 1826 by order of the magistrates and

---

[279] The Rev. J. Cox, *Three Centuries of Derbyshire Annals* (1890), vol 2, p. 43 describes gibbeting as 'a coarse custom very prevalent in medieval England.'

[280] *Derby Mercury*, March 13, 1815.

[281] The expenses of the gibbeting came to £85.4.1. and, in addition, the gaoler charged ten guineas for conveying the body from Derby to Wardlow.

Lingard's remains buried on the spot. The field where he lies is still known as gibbet field.[282]

The last man to be gibbeted in England was James Cook, a 22-year-old book-binder, who murdered a London tradesman. His body was hung in chains in Leicester in August 1832 in front of a crowd of some 20,000 people. Shortly afterwards the body was removed by order of the Under-Secretary of State. Gibbeting was abolished by statute in 1834.[283]

On Tuesday evening, a disturbance, trifling indeed in its commencement, but dreadful in its progress, and fatal in its consequences, happened in this town. The privates of Colonel Cameron's newly raised regiment refused to disperse after the evening exercise. The colonel remonstrated with them upon the impropriety of their conduct, but the men in return complained that part of their bounty money had been hitherto withheld, and arrears of their pay were due. Of the justice of this complaint we cannot pretend to speak; but in consequence of the circumstances, a number of people assembled in Norfolk Street and upon the parade. R.A. Althorpe esq., Colonel of the volunteers, who had been previously ordered to hold themselves in readiness, now appeared at their head, and, in a peremptory tone, commanded the people instantly to disperse, which not being immediately complied with, a person, who shall be nameless, plunged with his horse among the unarmed, defenceless people, and wounded with his sword men, women and children promiscuously. The people murmured and fell back in confusion. The Riot Act was read. The people ran to and fro, scarcely one in a hundred knowing what was meant by these dreadful measures; when, an hour being expired, the volunteers fired upon their townsmen with bullets, and killed two persons upon the spot; several others were wounded, and the rest fled on every side in consternation. The whole town was alarmed, and continued in a state of agitation all night long. It is our duty to say, that, during the whole of this bloody business, no violence was committed upon any man's person or property by the people, no symptoms of a riotous disposition were manifested, except by one enraged individual, who threw a few stones, by which several of the volunteers were bruised.

The article which earned James Montgomery six months' imprisonment in York Castle.

[282] L Radzinowicz, *A History of English Criminal Law*, Stevens & Son, London, 1948, vol. 1, p 218.
[283] Ibid., pp. 218-219.

The Clock, York Castle referred to in Montgomery's poem
'The Pleasures of Imprisonment Epistle II'.

The tombstones erected in memory of Mary Morgan in Presteigne Church-yard.

Appendix 6

The Judge and the Servant Girl [284]

When, in April, 1805 a jury at Brecon Great Sessions acquitted Mary Morris of the murder of her illegitimate child, the judge, 61-year-old George Hardinge, took no pains to hide his displeasure. As chance would have it, at Presteigne, the next county town on the Brecon circuit, there was another child murder case to try. The accused was 17-year-old Mary Morgan, a servant of Walter Wilkins, a JP and a former sheriff of Radnor. He and Hardinge knew each other well. Between 1784 and 1801 both had sat as MPs, their wives were cousins and, following his appointment as a Welsh judge in 1787, Hardinge had more than once enjoyed hospitality at Maesllwych Castle, Wilkins' palatial home at Glasbury-on-Wye. It is possible that he had seen Mary there and had eaten food which she had helped prepare.

In Spring 1804 Mary had discovered that she was pregnant. An attempted abortion having failed, she decided to kill the child as soon as it was born. She gave birth on the afternoon of Sunday 23 September. Using a penknife, which her lover had given her for the purpose, she immediately slit the baby's throat, almost severing its head from its body and hid the corpse under her mattress. 'I did so,' she would later explain, 'being perfectly sure I could not provide for it myself.' The crime was quickly discovered and two days later the county coroner held an inquest at the Castle. The jury brought in a verdict of murder and Mary was committed to the county gaol for trial at the next Great Sessions.

The man suspected of fathering the dead child was Wilkins' son Walter. Hardinge would later tell the Bishop of St Asaph in a letter that Walter was Mary's favourite gallant and had, upon learning that she was pregnant, offered to maintain the child when born if she would name him as the father. According to Hardinge, she had believed that he 'would save her by a letter to me.' If that was her hope, she was to be sorely disappointed. Not only did Walter Wilkins junior not intercede on her behalf, but he actually sat on the grand jury which found the bill of indictment against her. How he, or Hardinge, can have thought it proper that he sit on that jury beggars belief. Worse was to come. When Mary asked him for a guinea to fee counsel to defend her, he refused and, had not the high sheriff humanely intervened, she would have gone undefended.

Her trial commenced at 3 o'clock on the April 11, 1805. She was confident of acquittal and had ordered gay apparel to attest her deliverance. The townsfolk shared her belief and, as the trial proceeded, celebratory fireworks were set off in the street. The evidence did not take long to go through. Servants from the Castle who had testified before the coroner were called to repeat what they had said then. There were no witnesses for the defence. The evidence finished, Hardinge launched into his

---

[284] This case has been included principally because it comes from the same era as that of Mary Thorpe and bears more than a passing similarity to it.

summing up. He warned the jury against leniency: 'I am not afraid of telling you that offences like this are of late becoming prevalent and that a culprit has recently escaped her doom whose crime was in local vicinity and was near to the scene of this.' This jury did not disappoint but were quickly back with a verdict of guilty. In a long harangue Hardinge urged the terrified girl to seek God's forgiveness. He complained that it was hard to 'cut off a young creature like you in the morning of life's day. You must not think us cruel; it is to save other infants like yours and many other girls like you from the pit into which you are fallen; your sentence and your death is a mercy to them.' He then sentenced her to hang. Had he been so inclined, he could have recommended that she be pardoned on condition of transportation: she was young, and more, that he had been impressed by her modest demeanour at trial. But he did not. He had severe views on infanticide.

The execution was set for the morning of the 13th, which left no time for an application to London for a pardon. An outsider had to be brought in to drive the cart which carried Mary to the tree in Gallows Lane from which she was hanged, for no local man would help. She was buried in the yard of the parish church. The Earl of Ailesbury paid for a tombstone with an inscription commending Hardinge as a humane judge by whose words the dead girl had been roused to a sense of remorse and guilt. Close by it stands another erected by the town which reads 'In memory of Mary Morgan who suffered April 13th 1805 ... He that is without sin among you let him first cast a stone at her'.

In the course of his judicial career, Hardinge had sent and would send many of his fellow creatures to their deaths, but Mary's fate seems to have weighed on his conscience. Whenever he was in Presteigne he visited her grave. The visits inspired him to both a poem (*On Seeing The Tomb of Mary Morgan*) and a Latin epitaph. By a curious irony, as he had been the instrument of her death so was she of his. In Spring 1816, despite suffering from a chest cold, he made his by now customary pilgrimage. He collapsed at the graveside and within days was dead of pleurisy. One doubts if he was much missed by the common people. When, in 1815, he sentenced another Radnor woman to hang, some men of the town had shown what they thought of the sentence by breaking her out of Presteigne gaol and spiriting her away. Even Byron knew his reputation:

> 'There was this Waggish Welsh Judge ...
>
> In his great office so completely skilled
>
> That when a culprit came for condemnation
>
> He had his Judge's Joke for consolation.'

> *(Don Juan*, XIII).

185

Index

Index

Index